A-LEVEL YEAR 2

STUDENT GUIDE

OCR

Sociology

Debates in contemporary society

Globalisation and the digital social world

Option 1: Crime and deviance

Steve Chapman
Katherine Roberts

Hodder Education, an Hachette UK company, Blenheim Court, George Street, Banbury, Oxfordshire OX16 5BH

Orders

Bookpoint Ltd, 130 Park Drive, Milton Park, Abingdon, Oxfordshire OX14 4SB

tel: 01235 827827

fax: 01235 400401

e-mail: education@bookpoint.co.uk

Lines are open 9.00 a.m.–5.00 p.m., Monday to Saturday, with a 24-hour message answering service. You can also order through the Hodder Education website: www.hoddereducation.co.uk

ISBN 978-1-4718-5972-4

First printed 2016

Impression number 5 4 3 2 1

Year 2020 2019 2018 2017 2016

Acknowledgement

The authors and publisher would like to thank Laura Pountney for her contribution to this book.

Typeset by Integra Software Services Pvt. Ltd., Pondicherry, India

Printed in Italy

Cover photo: thakala/Fotolia

Contents

Getting the most from this book

Exam tips

Advice on key points in the text to help you learn and recall content, avoid pitfalls, and polish your exam technique in order to boost your grade.

Knowledge check

Rapid-fire questions throughout the Content Guidance section to check your understanding.

Knowledge check answers

1 Turn to the back of the book for the Knowledge check answers.

Summaries

- Each core topic is rounded off by a bullet-list summary for quick-check reference of what you need to know.

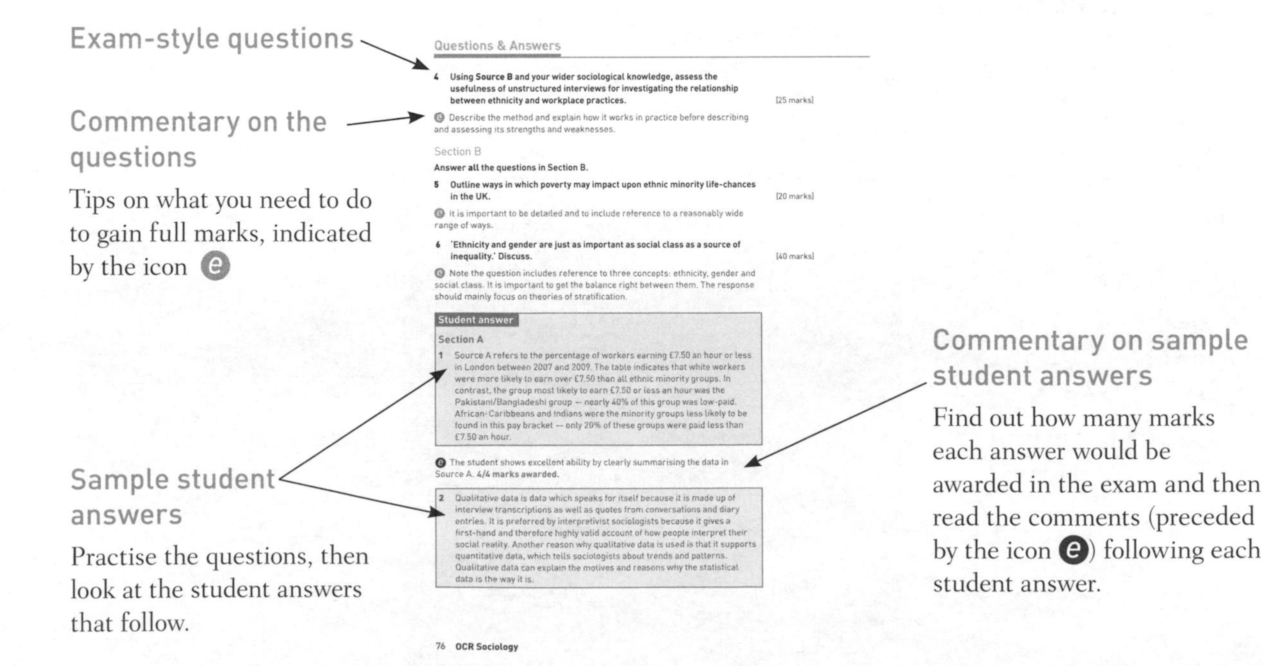

Questions & Answers

4 Using Source B and your wider sociological knowledge, assess the usefulness of unstructured interviews for investigating the relationship between ethnicity and workplace practices. [25 marks]

e Describe the method and explain how it works in practice before describing and assessing its strengths and weaknesses.

Section B

Answer all the questions in Section B.

5 Outline ways in which poverty may impact upon ethnic minority life-chances in the UK. [20 marks]

e It is important to be detailed and to include reference to a reasonably wide range of ways.

6 'Ethnicity and gender are just as important as social class as a source of inequality.' Discuss. [40 marks]

e Note the question includes reference to three concepts: ethnicity, gender and social class. It is important to get the balance right between them. The response should mainly focus on theories of stratification.

Student answer

Section A

1 Source A refers to the percentage of workers earning £7.50 an hour or less in London between 2007 and 2009. The table indicates that white workers were more likely to earn over £7.50 than all ethnic minority groups. In contrast, the group most likely to earn £7.50 or less an hour was the Pakistani/Bangladeshi group — nearly 40% of this group was low-paid. African-Caribbeans and Indians were the minority groups less likely to be found in this pay bracket — only 20% of these groups were paid less than £7.50 an hour.

e The student shows excellent ability by clearly summarising the data in Source A. **4/4 marks awarded.**

2 Qualitative data is data which speaks for itself because it is made up of interview transcriptions as well as quotes from conversations and diary entries. It is preferred by interpretivist sociologists because it gives a first-hand and therefore highly valid account of how people interpret their social reality. Another reason why qualitative data is used is that it supports quantitative data, which tells sociologists about trends and patterns. Qualitative data can explain the motives and reasons why the statistical data is the way it is.

76 **OCR Sociology**

About this book

This guide covers Component 3: Debates in contemporary society in the OCR A-level Sociology specification H580. It focuses on the compulsory topic Globalisation and the digital social world and the optional topic Crime and deviance.

How to use the book

The first main section of the book is **Content Guidance**. It follows the headings for Debates in contemporary society in the OCR specification, specifically the topics Globalisation and the digital social world and Crime and deviance. Each section of the Content Guidance contains exam tips, knowledge checks and definitions of some key terms. Knowing and understanding the meaning of sociological concepts is an essential part of the whole course.

The second main section of the book is **Questions & Answers**. At the beginning of this section is information about the A-level examination and the different sections of the exam paper for this component. The A-level questions provided are in the style of the OCR exam for Component 3 and are each followed by an A-grade answer. Following each student answer you will find comments explaining why what has been written is good and is scoring well. More detailed guidance on how to use the Questions & Answers section is given at the beginning of that section.

Content Guidance

Section A Globalisation and the digital social world

What is the relationship between globalisation and digital forms of communication?

Definitions of globalisation

Al-Rodhan (2015) points out that defining globalisation is anything but easy, while Ellwood describes the concept as 'the least understood concept of the new millennium'.

In 1964, Marshall McLuhan predicted the emergence of what he called the 'global village'. He likened communications and media in the 1960s to a giant central nervous system which ultimately would connect everybody in the world. He argued that this would eventually compress the world's thousands of cultures into one 'super-culture', predicting **cultural homogenisation** — the idea that cultural diversity would eventually be replaced by cultural sameness. McLuhan's idea of the global village can clearly be seen in modern definitions of globalisation.

Albrow, for example, defines globalisation as all those processes by which the disparate people of the world have been incorporated into a single society, while Waters observes that it is a social process in which the constraints of geography on economic, political, social and cultural arrangements have declined. At its simplest, globalisation means that the world we live in now feels smaller and more accessible than it was a decade ago.

Martell observes that, at a micro level, globalisation for individuals means that both geographical distance and time zones are no longer important. Harvey (1990) calls this space–time compression. The instantaneous interaction afforded by digital technology such as e-mails or instant messaging has erased distance and substituted virtual space for physical space. It doesn't matter where physically people are in the world; this global digital interconnectedness means people can occupy the same online space at the same time.

At a macro or societal level, globalisation means that goods, money, people, services, popular culture, drugs, crime, terror, disease, news, images, ideas, religions and pollution are now crossing national borders on an extraordinary scale and at an incredible speed. Societies that were once distant, independent and very different to one another, are today increasingly globally intertwined and interdependent whether they want to be or not. Moreover, the macro and micro are also interwoven in that the local lives of ordinary people everywhere in the world are increasingly shaped by events, decisions and actions that take place thousands of miles from where they live and work.

Exam tip

The examiner expects you to be aware of the various definitions of globalisation and to consider the problems in defining the concept.

Cultural homogenisation Refers to the reduction in cultural diversity across the world and its replacement with cultural sameness, especially in popular culture. A homogeneous world is one composed of elements that are all of the same kind or essentially alike. It is based on the idea that the more people consume the same films, music and brands, the more likely they are to feel connected despite distance. There may be a sense of global community based on similar cultural experience which may have the long-term effect of reducing cultural diversity.

Knowledge check 1

Explain what is meant by space–time compression.

The emergence of globalisation

Sociologists who argue in favour of globalisation argue that it has been brought about by the following.

Technological advances

Advances in digital forms of communication and computer technology, particularly e-mail, smartphones, satellite technology, digital television, texting and the internet (with its diversity of websites, social media networks and blogs), have transformed the world's concept of time, distance and space. Information in all its varied forms — news, political ideas and dissent, financial transactions and cultural products — can now be transmitted instantaneously to most global destinations from any part of the world that has a digital connection. For example, most banks, stock exchanges and trading markets have utilised digital technology to set up a 24-hour global financial market, while transnational businesses have used digital technology such as e-mails, conference calls and the internet to effectively manage an international division of labour in which production and marketing are often scattered across continents.

Digital communications have helped to globalise war, conflict and terrorism. For example, smartphones in Africa are seen as necessities in coordinating civil wars, while terrorist organisations such as al-Qaeda and ISIS have successfully used the internet and social networking sites to globally publicise their cause.

Ownership and control of digital media

Ownership and control of the world's digital forms of communication have become increasingly concentrated in the hands of fewer transnational corporations. This has resulted in cultural products such as films, television, music, designer fashion, news, social networking sites, food, drink, brands and sport being developed and manufactured for global rather than local consumption. Steven (2004) observes that, despite huge differences in distance and upbringing, much of the world's population now listens to the same music and watches the same films and television via the same digital communication networks and social media.

Other developments

Other important developments which may have contributed to a process of globalisation include the rapid growth of cheap air travel and mass tourism, as well as the continuing dominance of the English language in digital communication, particularly on the internet.

Exam tip

The micro–macro distinction is a useful evaluative tool. Don't just focus on the impact of globalisation on societies. Think also about its impact on individuals. For example, compare the impact of globalisation on your own life compared with someone living in a developing country.

Knowledge check 2

Identify three major reasons why some sociologists believe globalisation has occurred.

Developments in digital forms of communication in a global society

Digital revolution

Some sociologists argue that the social world can be divided into three revolutionary periods:

1 The agricultural revolution — the development of farming to cultivate crops.
2 The industrial revolution — the development of science and technology to build machinery in order to manufacture goods from raw materials in factories.

3 The computer or information age — the development of the internet or worldwide web. This global multimedia library of information and services in cyberspace is made possible by a global system of interconnected super-computers. The development of high-capacity broadband wireless networks means more people than ever can connect at high speed to this super-information highway and communicate in forms very different to those found in the pre-digital age such as physically chatting with a friend, talking on the telephone, sending a fax or writing a letter. For example, Skype means that users can see and chat to other people on the other side of the world.

The early twenty-first century saw a further revolution in communication as society entered a digital age. Digitalisation refers to a dramatic change in the way information is stored and transmitted. All information, regardless of format (for example, images, text and sound) is now converted into binary code. This led to an explosion of new types of digital communication devices including cheap laptop computers, tablets, smartphones and digital television.

Digitalisation led to three types of **media convergence**:

- **Technological convergence** refers to the fact that digitalisation has led to the merging of different types of information — text, photographs, video, film, voices, maps, e-mail, music and social networking — into a single delivery system or digital communication device such as smart televisions, laptops, tablets and smartphones. Digitalisation now allows information to be delivered immediately across a range of media platforms which were once separate and unconnected technologies.
- **Economic convergence** refers to the fact that media, computer, television and telecommunications companies that once operated in separate spheres of development and production are increasingly engaging in technological and economic alliances with one another to produce multimedia delivery systems. This is because digitalisation has rendered the borders between these forms of communication irrelevant.
- **Cultural convergence** refers to the fact that most members of society increasingly interact with one another using the same type of digital communication. Old ways of communicating such as writing letters are gradually being replaced by digital social media networks such as Facebook, Snapchat, Instagram and Twitter. Cultural convergence means that the way people consume is changing too. For example, six out of ten British adults now use the internet to buy products such as food, clothing, music, insurance and holidays.

Exam tip

It is important not to judge the pre-digital era as inferior. It is merely different and can be used to evaluate the importance of digital media. For example, are old forms of media such as newspapers and television really redundant?

A major feature of the digital age has been the appearance and rapid spread of social media platforms. Social media refers to a participatory culture or network of websites and applications which enable a community of users to interact and collaborate. This participatory culture enables users to create and share content, to engage in social networking and to spread news. There are different types of social media, for example:

- Digital social networks, which encourage registered users to create public profiles and make lists of users who can be invited to share connections, upload photos and videos, send messages and keep in touch with friends, family and colleagues via computers, tablets and smartphones.

The most popular social networking site in the world is Facebook. In the USA, web users spend more time on Facebook than any other website, while in the UK Facebook is the default setting for 96% of adults who are online, according to a 2014 Ofcom survey. According to its official ethos, Facebook aims to make the world a more connected, open and empathetic place by encouraging people to share their social profile (identity and status), interests, feelings and so on and to maximise connectedness by accumulating friends and likes.

- Microblogging sites such as Twitter, which has 500 million users worldwide.
- Sites run by individual diarists and commentators known as bloggers, who write about a diversity of subjects from baking to politics.
- Video bloggers or vloggers, who upload videos of themselves onto YouTube, discussing commercial products relating to beauty or fashion, for example. Many of these are sponsored by advertisers.
- Open content sites such as Wikipedia, on which users are encouraged to collaborate on an online web encyclopaedia.
- Social news forums such as Reddit, on which stories are socially curated, promoted and discussed by site members.
- Global conference sites such as TED talks, which are devoted to spreading academic ideas.
- Virtual-world sites such as CyberCity, Second Life and World of Warcraft, which enable users to live alternative lives in alternative virtual worlds. For example, Second Life has over a million global users. Participants create virtual 3-D representations of themselves called avatars, who are able to interact, socialise, trade and even have sex with other avatars.

Before the computer/digital age, people who wished to share their interests, ideas or opinions with people in other parts of the country or world were constrained by geographical distance, time zones and forms of communication that were either slow (letters) or expensive (telephones). However, the computer/digital age has produced **virtual communities** in which globally dispersed people with common interests are no longer constrained by geographical distance or time zones. The existence of the internet and its diversity of websites, newsgroups, discussion boards, social networking platforms and so on, as well as e-mail and video applications such as Skype, has produced instantaneous interaction and sharing at any time and from any place.

Virtual communities Communities that exist on the internet.

Van Dijk argues that both identity and community are increasingly shaped by these virtual communities. For example, he observes that teenagers can no longer imagine organising their social lives without Facebook at its centre; news organisations have become increasingly dependent on Twitter for breaking news stories; would-be pop superstars ignore YouTube at their peril, while A-level students cannot imagine an academic world without Google and Wikipedia. Carter argues that members of virtual communities see the relationships that they establish online as equally important to those that they establish in offline physical communities.

Networked global society

This concept is mainly associated with the Marxist sociologist Manuel Castells, who argued that in the twenty-first century people are more likely to be organised into horizontal digital communication networks using new forms of social media than in the traditional vertical organisations of the past. Moreover, these networks connect people and allow them to be interactive at the speed of light. Digital technologies have therefore transformed all relationships whether they are personal, political, religious, cultural or economic.

For example, politics used to involve either joining vertical organisations such as a political party or pressure group and/or reading the products of such organisations, for example political manifestos. In addition, media organisations, which were also vertical organisations, attempted to influence voters. Consequently, political news or scandal travelled relatively slowly.

However, in contrast, Castells argues that new digital media such as Twitter, Facebook, blogs and websites have transformed not only the relationship that the electorate now has with politicians but also the way that politicians now behave — political news and gossip is instantaneously available via these new media networks and can ruin political careers within minutes. Moreover, these networks are global too, so people's political interests now often extend beyond domestic politics to how Britain engages with the rest of the world.

Knowledge check 3

Explain the difference between a traditional vertical organisation and a horizontal digital network, using religion as the context.

Exam tip

Although the specification is not specifically asking you to explore theories such as functionalism, the New Right and interactionism, it is still useful to think about how these theories would interpret new forms of digital communication. You could use them as evaluation of Marxist, feminist and postmodernist theories.

Applying sociological theories to digital forms of communication

Marxism

Marxist ideas about digital and social media constitute a critical digital sociology. Fuchs, for example, generally takes a conflict view of the role of digital communication in reproducing and legitimating inequality in capitalist society.

Fuchs observes that Karl Marx argued that 'the ideas of the ruling class are in every epoch the ruling ideas … The class which has the means of material production at its disposal, has control at the same time over the means of mental production, so … the ideas of those who lack the means of mental production are subject to it.' Marxist theories of the media and the newer digitalised forms of communication therefore generally argue that all forms of communication are ideological in that they function on behalf of the capitalist ruling class to reproduce and justify class inequality. Marxists believe that the role of digital social media (along with other ideological agencies, such as traditional media, education and religion) is to bring about a state of 'false class consciousness' so that citizens do not criticise or challenge the unequal and unjust organisation of capitalist society.

Knowledge check 4

What do Marxists mean when they say all forms of digital communication are ideological?

Marxists argue that the popularity of social media such as Facebook functions to reinforce false class consciousness because digital social networks mainly focus on non-critical issues such as identity, entertainment and consumption, and consequently are rarely important vehicles of protest and social change. Those who own or control these new forms of communication and social networks aim to shape and manipulate how people think about the world they live in so that they only get a narrow range of 'approved' views and knowledge, with the result that 'alternative' and critical points of view are rarely heard or are dismissed altogether as extremist.

Seabrook sees the globalisation linked to digital communication as a type of **cultural imperialism** because it is dominated by Western cultural industries which use digital forms of communication to impose their cultural values on the rest of the world. He argues that integration into a single global economy and culture is a 'declaration of

Cultural imperialism Refers to the ability of richer nations and some global corporations to impose their cultural products on the rest of the world. It is often argued that cultural imperialism leads to cultural homogenisation.

cultural war' upon other cultures. It implies that traditional cultures have little or no value. Seabrook argues that this cultural imperialism attempts to replace diversity with homogenisation and this often results in painful social and religious disruption as local cultures attempt to resist. Some observers have suggested that the recent growth in Islamist fundamentalism may be a reaction to these processes.

Marxists often point to six factors which they claim support their case:

1. Digital forms of communication are merely a continuation of older forms of media and consequently are subject to the same economic and social influences. Cornford and Robins (1999) argue that the so-called new media are not that 'new'. Older forms of technology such as telephone landlines are still integral to the use of new digital communication, for example broadband connections to the internet. They argue that the only thing that is new about digital media is speed — information, news and entertainment can be accessed in 'real time'. Cornford and Robins suggest that what the new technologies permit is the refinement, extension and embellishment of traditional media.

2. Jenkins argues that most new forms of digital media have developed as a result of investment by the big media corporations and consequently ownership of digital communications is concentrated in the hands of a few major transnational corporations. In particular, he argues that owning different types of media made it more desirable for companies to develop content across a variety of media platforms and delivery systems. As Jenkins notes, 'digitalisation set the conditions for convergence; corporate conglomerates created its imperative'.

   An examination of the internet suggests that it is dominated by a small number of media corporations — for example, Microsoft has developed most of the software required for accessing the net, while Google is the most popular search engine. Apple and Samsung dominate the smartphone market. Most of the internet's commercially viable content is therefore controlled and/or commissioned by a handful of media conglomerates.

3. Digital forms of communication are becoming increasingly commercialised. In particular, in the last 10 years there has been a major shift in internet activities, from educational use to commercial use. Advertising has become a central feature of most social networking sites. Technologies such as **cookies** can monitor and process the data generated by interactive media usage, so they can segment and target potential future audiences, and thus enhance profits.

4. Marxists such as Fuchs point out that those who participate in the new digital culture are not created equal. Corporations, governments — and even individuals within corporate media — exert greater power than aggregates of consumers or those with genuine political and economic grievances. They suggest that digital technologies and networks mainly strengthen the power of existing elites and, in so doing, they contribute to the 'muting' of those — the politically and economically repressed — who have genuine grievances with the way capitalism is organised.

Knowledge check 5

Why do Cornford and Robins argue that new forms of digital media are not that new?

Cookie Information that a website puts on your computer hard drive so that it can remember something about you at a later time.

Knowledge check 6

What do Marxists mean by 'muting'?

5 Castells has highlighted the global criminal economy, which overlaps with the legitimate global economy. It is worth at least £1 trillion a year and has been made possible by digital forms of communication.
6 Marxist critical thinkers such as McChesney highlight the similarity of digital content and social networking. Facebook, Google and Twitter, for example, operate in hundreds of countries across the world. McChesney claims such companies are like imperial powers colonising the minds of millions of people across the world so they behave and think in the same way. He argues that this 'cult of homogeneity', which speaks to everyone in general and no one in particular, crowds out local cultural products. He claims that it has also reduced people's opportunity to speak out, that is, it has silenced or muted less powerful groups so that they are less likely to challenge issues such as inequality or to speak out against injustice.

Exam tip

Think about using examples of the types of global crime that might be facilitated by digital communication — for example, identity theft, tax fraud, pornography and terrorism.

However, this Marxist account of digital communications has been challenged for the following reasons.

- It assumes a unified conspiracy on the part of the providers of digital forms of communication. However, the owners of digital forms of communication are not united because their companies are involved in competition with one another for a bigger share of the market and therefore profit.
- Marxists tend to overemphasise social class at the expense of other inequalities that may also result in **muted voices** such as those relating to ethnicity, gender and sexuality.
- Neo-Marxists argue that ideas can exist independently of capitalism — these are not always the ideas of the ruling class and consequently do not always have to be ideological. Some Marxist observers of digital communications such as Castells have therefore argued that new media technologies and networks can revitalise democracy. It is argued that because the internet enables 'many to many' communication, it is capable of giving a voice to 'muted' groups such as the poor, the politically repressed, women, ethnic minorities, disabled people and the LGBT community, and encouraging greater community involvement in political action. It therefore gives a voice to those who would otherwise go unheard. It gives oppressed people the ability to come together and facilitate social change.

Muted voices Powerless social groups who are repressed or exploited. They are often prevented from speaking out and voicing their concerns.

Feminism

Feminist theory has traditionally focused on how societies tend to be organised in patriarchal ways, that is, in favour of men. Males dominate positions of power in most societies and consequently women in contrast generally occupy subordinate positions.

Feminists are usually critical of both old media and digital forms of communication, which they see as patriarchal agencies which mainly engage in the symbolic annihilation of women, that is, they tend to show women in a narrow and limited range of social roles and to suggest that their achievements are less important than their looks and bodies. A good example of this with regard to digital communication is the popularity of pornography websites on the internet. Feminists also point out that control of the content of new digital forms of communication is in the hands of transnational corporations mainly owned by men.

Knowledge check 7

Why are feminists critical of both old media and digital forms of communication?

Feminists were responsible for the development of 'muted group theory', which suggests groups with little power or status are muted or silenced by more powerful groups. Feminists argued that women were often unable to voice their concerns about patriarchy because a male-dominated media suppressed or muted them. Kramarae extended this argument to the internet, which, she observes, is constructed and mainly controlled by men despite the fact that women use it as much as men do. She argues that the companies controlling the digital technology that underpins cybercommunication, the way the internet is organised, much of its software and even the metaphors used to describe the internet such as the 'super-information highway' are masculine and that this has the effect of 'muting' the voice of women.

Knowledge check 8

Who controls the internet, according to Kramarae?

However, some feminists are positive about the power of digital forms of communication to change women's social position in society for the better. Haraway argues that the anonymity granted by many forms of digital communication allows people to transcend an oppressed identity such as being female and to take on an alternative identity which avoids the negative judgements and stereotypes often applied to feminine identity. Internet and chat-room IDs and blog names can be asexual. The online visual community Second Life, in which users create a utopian world, is a particularly good example of how people might transcend their gender identity. Users construct an avatar — an image that represents them — from a selection of generic choices including buff male bodies, voluptuous female forms and asexual humanoid alternatives such as **cyborgs**. Sociological research on Second Life users suggests they do not feel limited by their real gender identities when choosing an avatar identity. For example, some women reported that they had deliberately chosen to adopt male bodies in order to experience a masculine identity, while other women preferred the cyborg identity because interaction with others excluded sexual politics.

Cyborg In the context of digital communications, refers to a gender-neutral cyber-identity.

Cochrane identifies a fourth wave of feminism which, she argues, is powered by digital technology which is encouraging women to build an empowering, popular and reactive feminist movement online. In other words, women's voices are no longer muted. Green and Singleton argue that digital technology and particularly the internet is a feminine technology that has the potential to destabilise patriarchy because its use allows women to explore, subvert and create new identities and to resist sexist representations wherever they might occur. A good example of this online empowerment is Laura Bates's 'Everyday Sexism' project, which in 2015 had 108,000 followers on Twitter and Facebook. This is a consciousness-raising initiative which encourages women to send in their everyday experiences of street harassment, sexual harassment especially on public transport, workplace discrimination and the **body shaming** that they encounter.

Body shaming Refers to criticising individuals (usually women) because they do not conform to 'ideal' body shapes as defined by men, for example, women may be shamed for being 'fat'.

Cochrane observes that women are using digital forms of communication to protest about pornography, page 3 of *The Sun* newspaper, violence against women, the sexualisation of childhood and so on. Cochrane argues that digital technology has resulted in contemporary young women adopting an 'intersectional' form of feminism in which they are aware of how multiple oppressions — class inequality, poverty, race, age, sexuality, gender, ability, violence and so on — intersect to bring about **misogyny** and patriarchal institutions.

Knowledge check 9

What is an intersectional form of feminism?

Green and Singleton emphasise the central use of the smartphone and particularly texting in the creation and maintenance of feminine identities, friendship networks and communities across local and global spaces.

Misogyny Refers to dislike or hatred of women.

However, evidence suggests that women who use digital forms of communication may still be subjected to sexism, abuse and threats. For example, women who use new media such as the internet may experience the sorts of everyday sexism experienced in older forms of media. For example, women's rights campaigner Caroline Criado-Perez was subjected to online rape and murder threats in 2013, while the academic Mary Beard and the MP Stella Creasy have also received threats and sexist abuse via Twitter. The internet may help disseminate feminist ideas more widely but it also does the same for its polar opposite — woman-hating views.

Some critics have also argued that the fourth wave of digital feminism might be exaggerated in terms of its influence on women. Moreover, Green and Singleton suggest that the online communities that are most popular with women users — Mumsnet and Facebook — might merely reinforce the patriarchal notion that women should perform the emotional work of maintaining family relationships.

Exam tip

Another way of evaluating is to apply different feminist perspectives to digital forms of communication. For example, are radical feminists going to agree with Marxist feminists on the role of such technology?

Postmodernism

Postmodernists see digital forms of communication as beneficial because they argue that global digital networks are primarily responsible for diffusing different cultural styles around the world and creating new global hybrid styles in fashion, food, music, consumption and lifestyle. It is argued that in the postmodern world this cultural diversity will become the global norm. Postmodernists therefore see globalisation as a positive phenomenon because it has created a new class of global consumers, in both the developed and the developing world, with a greater range of choices from which they can construct a **hybridised global identity**.

Hybridised global identity Refers to the idea that in an increasingly hybridised world a person's beliefs or behaviour may be influenced by a mixture of the local and the global, and the traditional and the modern. For example, people who use global and modern social networking sites such as Facebook may continue to subscribe to traditional beliefs and local customs, although some of the latter may be modified by their social media experience.

Postmodernists make the following claims.

- Postmodern societies are media-saturated societies — new forms of digital communication therefore merely reflect the postmodern condition.
- Postmodern societies are underpinned by globalisation — media transnationals have used digital communications technology such as the internet and satellite television to remove the distinction between the global and the local and to increase consumer choice in the range of knowledge and entertainment available for consumption.
- The diversity of digital forms of communication has undermined explanations that claimed absolute truths (for example, world views provided by mainstream religions, science, political movements and so on). It has resulted in the fragmentation of knowledge and encouraged people to see that there are multiple interpretations or truths — all of which have some relative value.
- People are no longer content to inherit fixed identities imposed from without, such as social class or gender identity. Instead social media networks and virtual communities offer people a plurality of identities from which to choose and consume and so subvert traditional forms of identity.
- Audiences are immersed in so much information in the digital postmodern age that they find it difficult to distinguish between real life and the digital version of reality, which Baudrillard calls '**hyper-reality**'. This has led to some concerns about how people use digital forms of communication and whether such forms of communication are healthy for identity and relationships.

Hyper-reality Refers to the simulation or copy of reality such as that found in places like Disneyland or in films. Some postmodernists argue that people find it increasingly difficult to distinguish between reality and hyper-reality.

However, postmodern ideas about digital communication can be criticised because they often fail to recognise inequalities in access to such technology. Consequently, postmodernism fails to offer any explanation for why some groups experience a **digital divide** and 'muted voice' despite the diversity of choice available in digital forms of communication. Postmodernists probably exaggerate the impact of the 'digital information explosion' on ordinary people's capacity to bring about change in their social identities and lives.

Digital divide Refers to inequalities in access to and use of digital technologies. For example, some people cannot afford to invest in smartphones.

Summary

- There is no universal agreement on how to define globalisation, whether it is actually occurring or, if it is, what its causes are.
- It is accepted that the rapid advances in digital technology in the past 20 years have compressed distance in space and time. Instantaneous communication with any part of the world at any time has had the effect of making the world seem a smaller place.
- Marxists generally see global processes such as digital social networks as ideological because ownership of digital media is concentrated in the hands of a small number of media corporations. Marxists argue that digital social networks are generally geared to reproducing and legitimating capitalism although Castells believes that a networked global society can produce a new type of popular politics that can bring about real social change.
- Feminists see the internet and digital communication as a positive weapon against misogyny and patriarchy.
- Postmodernists see the globalisation of digital communications as positive because they argue it will produce more cultural diversity as hybrid cultures emerge.

What is the impact of digital forms of communication in a global context?

The impact of digital forms of communication

Social inequalities

Some sociologists are concerned about what has been described as a digital divide, that is, inequalities are apparent in terms of who has access to digital forms of communication, particularly computers, broadband and internet access, and smartphones. In particular, access to and use of digital communication and being regularly and positively connected to others in networks bring about **social capital**. Conversely some groups may be denied access to such social capital.

Social capital Refers to the emotional, psychological, social and economic benefits that derive from being a member of a group or digital network.

The generational divide

The quick-moving nature of the digital world means that younger users come of age in a vastly different media environment than those who were born just a few years apart and this makes it difficult to ascertain whether there is a generational divide in the use of digital communications. When digital technology first took off in the 1990s, it was probably true that the older generation, that is, the 50+ age group, was left behind by a so-called '**net generation**'. However, in the twenty-first century, micro-generation gaps are now apparent, with each group of children uniquely influenced by the latest digital tools available in their formative stages of development.

Exam tip

Pick up marks for interpretation skills by giving examples of social capital for groups such as young people or the elderly.

Prensky refers to these young people as '**digital natives**' because the internet is a 'natural' environment into which they are fully integrated. Fluency in digital culture is second nature to them and they feel a strong sense of community when online. Most of them are confident users of multiple devices on which they multitask.

Digital natives Refers to people who have used digital communications since their early childhood and consequently are naturally skilled in the use of digital devices and software.

Research suggests that those in the **net generation** who are now in their mid-30s and early-40s still spend time talking on their smartphones, still watch television and use e-mail frequently. However, the micro-generation of the early to mid-2000s — the so-called **iGeneration** — spends considerably more time texting than talking on the phone, tends to communicate more over instant-messenger networks and are more likely to be involved in active and regular engagement with the internet, for example uploading, blogging and networking. It may be the case that the next micro-generation of digital communication users will be very different from their older siblings because the technology is evolving so swiftly.

Net generation Refers to the first generation of internet users in the 1990s.

iGeneration Refers to those born after 2000.

The 2015 Ofcom survey suggests that the macro-generational divides between young and middle-aged or elderly users may now be in decline as older age groups (digital immigrants) increasingly engage in online activities such as social networking via smartphones and tablets.

Knowledge check 10

What is the difference between the net generation and the iGeneration?

The digital class divide

Some sociologists such as Helsper have argued that digital communications are dominated by middle-class usage because this social class can afford to invest in the most recent digital technology. In contrast, it is argued that the revolution in digital communications has created a **digital underclass** because the poor lack the resources to join in with this new media usage. Helsper claims that this digital underclass is characterised by unemployment, lower education levels and low digital skills.

Digital underclass Refers to those who cannot afford or do not have the skills to use digital forms of communication.

Evidence suggests that although the digital class divide has narrowed in recent years, it still exists. For example, surveys demonstrate that the so-called digital underclass has increased its use of the internet at a much slower rate than other social groups and those members of this group that do have internet access rate their skills as poorer than other more educated groups. The 2015 Ofcom survey also found that 95% of the AB socioeconomic group use a range of new media devices to go online in any location compared with only 75% of the DE socioeconomic group and 86% of all socioeconomic groups. Three-quarters of ABs own a smartphone compared to only 54% of DEs.

A gendered digital divide

Li and Kirkup (2007) found significant gender differences between men and women in the UK in their use of digital communication. Men were more likely than women to use e-mail or chat rooms, and men played more computer games on consoles such as the X-Box than women. Ofcom (2015) reported that in 2014 adult males in the UK accessed the internet for an average of 23.3 hours per week compared with 17.8 hours for adult females. Women (67%) were slightly more likely than men (60%) to go online and to use social media sites.

The global divide

According to the World Bank, in 2012, about three-quarters of the world's population had access to a mobile phone. There are now 6 billion mobile subscriptions in use worldwide, of which nearly 5 billion are in developing countries. However, the West still has greater access to mobile broadband and the internet than the less developed world.

Mobile phone use has spread particularly quickly in Africa. In 2014, it was estimated that 72% of Africans use mobile phones. However, there are regional disparities in access to mobile phones — for example, in Eritrea, only 5% of the population owns a mobile phone while over 70% of people in South Africa, Nigeria and Kenya have such phones.

Smartphones (those that can access the internet and applications) are less widely used. Only 18% of Africans had access to a smartphone in 2014 although significant minorities own these devices in several nations, including 34% of South Africans and 27% of Nigerians (compared with 64% of Americans).

Furthermore, only 7% of Africa's inhabitants are online. This is because mobile connectivity in Africa is limited. Again, digital connectivity is highest in South Africa and Nigeria. Difficulties of access to the internet are also compounded by the fact that most of the language of the world wide web is English and the fact that a fairly large proportion of people in African countries are illiterate.

Knowledge check 11

Identify three reasons why a digital divide exists in Africa.

People's identity

Social networking platforms such as Facebook have become the most important infrastructure through which people organise their lives and interact with others in the twenty-first century. In particular, Facebook has become the major agency for packaging, promoting and presenting the self for public consumption. People use Facebook (and other social media platforms like Twitter, Snapchat and Instagram) to project their identity out into the world; to show who they are. Virtual-world sites such as Second Life enable people to choose alternative identities. All in all, then, new forms of digital communication have given people greater choice in selecting and constructing the identity that they want to present to the wider world.

Van Dijk argues that people have a vested interest in what Castells calls '**mass self-communication**' because they subscribe to the view that disclosing information about their identity is closely associated with popularity. Identity is therefore a social product constructed by members of social networks for consumption by others in return for admiration and social approval. According to Turkle, internet-based social networks free people of the burdens of their physical identities and allow them to present 'better' versions of themselves.

Mass self-communication Refers to use of social networking sites like Facebook to communicate information about ourselves to hundreds or thousands of people.

An interesting dimension of digital media is the fact that millions of people like to construct new identities for themselves in online virtual worlds. Boellstorff has conducted research into Second Life, which is the most popular of these worlds, and found that the experience of virtual worlds can reshape ideas about people's identity. For example, both men and women users of Second Life may experiment with identity by adopting avatars of the opposite sex to their real-life selves or by adopting gender-neutral cyborg identities. Similarly, Carter's research on another virtual community, CyberCity, observes that users see their online identities as just as important as their offline identities, and that friendships made online often migrate into the real world.

Knowledge check 12

Identify two research findings with regard to identity that research by Boellstorff and Carter discovered.

Youth and identity

Gardner and Davis observe that young people are the most frequent users of social media. Van Dijk claims social networking sites have replaced e-mail and the phone as the preferred mode of interaction for teenagers. Gardner and Davis's research indicates that young people take a great deal of care in how they present themselves online for public consumption. They identify three trends in this **presentation of self**:

1. Many young people construct a socially desirable and polished self online. This 'glammed-up' online identity generally exaggerates the more socially attractive aspects of the person's personality but downplays less 'cool' traits. This generally means that a young person's online identity may be more outgoing and extroverted than their offline everyday identity.
2. Some young people adopt a range of fictitious identities because they want to represent themselves in different ways on different sites. They are responding to different audiences who may have different expectations. For example, a person may construct a Facebook identity to attract maximum connectedness, a Twitter identity which is 'edgy' in its commentary on events, an avatar identity in Second Life which has characteristics that the user lacks in real life and a Reddit identity which is deliberately intended to provoke other people.
3. Once the self has been constructed on a social networking platform like Facebook, there is evidence that young people then engage in **identity performance** in that free time is mainly taken up checking phones in order to manage the online impressions others have of them by 'liking' what others upload as well as updating their own profile and status.

Presentation of self Refers to the public persona that we project to the world via social networking sites. We may, for example, exaggerate aspects of our real selves and be partial in what we tell the world about ourselves.

Identity performance Refers to the ways we attempt to manage and control other people's impressions of us.

Knowledge check 13

In what ways do young people present themselves on social networking sites?

Some observers have suggested that young people's obsession with their digital or virtual identity has created a number of modern-day problems.

- Gardner and Davis argue that this constant self-projection and self-tracking online reduces the time teenagers have for self-contemplation and real-life interaction with others. They observe that the maintenance of virtual identity means that teenagers are more **narcissistic** compared with previous generations.
- Twenge argues that fear of negative reaction to their identity performance is producing rising levels of moodiness, anxiety, sadness and isolation among teenagers.
- Turkle suggests that young people are mentally 'tethered' to their digital devices, as symbolised by their need to constantly track and check their connections. She argues that this has weakened young people's ability to develop an autonomous sense of self. They are too dependent on how other people react to them online. She claims that it is as if their thoughts and feelings are not real until they have been validated by others online.

Narcissism Refers to excessive love or admiration of ourselves.

The elderly and identity

There are signs that the greater take-up of digital communication by older people may have benefits for their self-esteem and identity. Researchers who carried out a study of elderly people's use of social media in Britain and Italy found that training older vulnerable people to use social media improves their cognitive capacity, increases a sense of self-competence and could have a beneficial overall impact on their mental health and physical well-being. Researchers found that the majority of their sample who had the hardware and the know-how reported feeling less isolated because of the digital connections they could make with relatives, friends and people with shared interests.

Exam tip

Note that most of the benefits identified in this section are examples of social capital.

Disability and identity

Ginsburg argues that interactive digital technologies provide powerful platforms for people with disabilities because they enable them to engage in first-person discussion of their worlds and experiences. There are three broad ways in which disabled people have used digital media to establish online identity:

1. Digital video activism — there has been an explosion of YouTube blogs featuring people with a range of disabilities encompassing autism to wheelchair use. The net sum of this has been to create a community in which those who have difficulty in face-to-face conversation and those who may be restricted to a particular identity can speak to an audience about their experience of disability.
2. Miller observes that Facebook has been used by people with disabilities to create support networks such as Disability Rights UK, Dancing Giraffe and Ableize, which aim to provide the 50,000 diverse disabled people in the UK with a voice and political influence by connecting them to each other online.
3. Many people with disabilities use virtual-world sites such as Second Life or Virtual Ability. Boellstorff observes that Second Life enables disabled people to take control of identity and their interactions with others by adopting virtual identities that are denied to them in real life. For example, people dependent on wheelchairs in real life can adopt avatars which walk, run and dance, while text chat equalises deaf people's ability to talk to everyone compared with the real world in which only a minority of non-disabled people are familiar with sign language. Virtual Ability has been designed by people with disabilities as a virtual community of support. It provides opportunities for disabled people to virtually experience a range of activities that they are excluded from in the real world, such as dancing, mountain climbing, trampolining and skydiving, in order to improve confidence, self-esteem and social skills.

However, although participation in the digital world by disabled people has considerably increased, the design of most digital media can also be disabling. For example, small fonts can be a problem for the visually impaired, while typing may not be possible for others.

Relationships

Digital social media in all its forms facilitate human interaction and relationships by constructing a **participatory culture**. Turkle (2011) refers to new-media users as 'cyborgs' because they are always connected to one other, regardless of where they are, via their laptops, tablets and smartphones. Gardner and Davis also observe that internet-enabled digital devices have enabled relationships because they transcend geographical and temporal barriers. They allow for immediacy of communication with others.

Participatory culture
A culture in which we are invited to connect to each other because we share the same interests or we wish to acquire various types of social capital or supports.

Young people, in particular, have taken advantage of digital technology to engage in frequent on-the-run communication with friends. In the UK over 90% of 16–24 year-olds send at least one text per day, while 73% also use social networking sites to send messages and maintain relationships. The average UK person sends 50 texts per week although this is small compared to the 'typical' teen, who sends up to 60 texts per day. Gardner and Davis suggest that young people now 'hang out' at Facebook (as they once did in physical places like cafes or McDonalds).

Several advantages of online relationships have been identified by Van Dijk as well as Gardner and Davis. Accumulating connections or online relationships is empowering and enriching because it produces social capital. Social capital broadly refers to the resources accumulated through relationships among people. This means that it has collective value for all concerned because connections and the opportunities which result from them are shared and reciprocated. For example:

- Membership of an online community may provide opportunities for people with similar interests to find and interact with one another. This type of capital is known as 'bonding social capital' and produces shared information flows that may throw up opportunities for jobs or mutual aid. For example, belonging to a Facebook community of A-level sociology students may bring benefits in terms of shared information about how to pass the exam.
- Membership of a particular online community may lead to relationships being established with others who are very different. This is known as 'bridging social capital'. For example, feminists may wish to bond with other feminists but social networking sites such as Twitter may lead to feminists realising that seemingly different political causes focused on aspects of inequality may in fact have a great deal in common with their cause. This may lead to political alliances which increase the potential for social change.
- Online texting and Facebooking function to micro-coordinate activity among friends. Gardner and Davis suggest digital communication is used as a 'virtual tap on the shoulder', establishing and maintaining links between friends who are physically separated. Cummings found that e-mail, instant messaging and social networking sites helped students stay in frequent contact with friends and family when separated by geography. Miller observes that, thanks to Facebook, people can maintain friendships over distance with less expenditure of time or money. He argues that use of social media extends existing relationships which may be weak because of distance or because they have lapsed over time and develops them into more meaningful relationships.
- Texting and social networking may function simply to fill time and alleviate boredom.
- Sites like Facebook may be a social lifeline, particularly for isolated, shy or disabled individuals, to stay connected to other people. Bargh and McKenna found that social platforms can help those with low self-esteem relate to others because they lower barriers to interaction (for example, it is not face-to-face) and this may make it easier for some people to disclose their feelings to others. Similarly, Gardner and Davis suggest texting and instant messaging is more private, intimate and less risky for sharing information about oneself.
- Social media enable minority groups that have traditionally been denied a voice in the traditional media — known as 'muted voices' — such as those with disabilities or ethnic minorities or tribal groups to create supportive communities that can highlight their everyday experience and coordinate activism.

- Online relationships may compensate for the fact that youth today have limited geographical freedom, enjoy less free time and are subject to more parental rules.
- Social media can positively change how people work. For example, thousands of people including this author use digital technology to work from home. This practice may benefit family life.
- Boyd argues that young people's involvement in public digital networks helps them to manage the transition from adolescence to adult society and assists their understanding of how to successfully negotiate public life. This is possible because sites like Facebook mirror and magnify both the positive and negative aspects of public everyday life.

Knowledge check 14

Identify three types of social capital that derive from relationships on social networking sites such as Facebook.

Criticisms of social networks

Critics of social networks suggest that the costs of this online revolution may outweigh the benefits. It is argued that digital forms of communication are actually bad for relationships for the following reasons:

1 Marxists such as Fuchs argue that it is the powerful who control digital communication and social media, and this undermines the concept of a participatory digital culture. Fuchs argues that as a result connectedness is less important than connectivity. Van Dijk illustrates this when he observes that the **algorithms** developed by social networking sites like Facebook for commercial reasons increasingly determine what people like, want, know or find. The aim of these algorithms is not to connect people but to keep them online as long as possible and to maximise the possibility that they will click on and connect to other commercial sites. Fuchs argues that friendship and connectedness have become commodified. Social media activity is not as voluntary as people believe it to be. Algorithms shepherd people towards making 'choices' that benefit capitalist agencies such as advertisers. Social media content may therefore simply reflect capitalist ideology.

Algorithm A list of digital rules that computers follow in order to identify connections between things. If you buy a book from Amazon, an algorithm works out what other books you may like and recommends them to you.

2 There are concerns about how the data collected by sites such as Facebook might be used. Facebook has already been accused of violating the privacy of its users. Other sites have used cookies to keep their users under surveillance.

There is also evidence that criminals are targeting social media and/ or using digital media to commit cybercrimes such as **identity theft**. It is becoming apparent to politicians and law-makers that new forms of social media (as well as their content) are very difficult to police.

Identity theft Occurs when criminals access their victims' personal information and then use it for their own gain.

3 The quality of online relationships or 'friends' has been questioned. Turkle observes that people boast about how many people they have 'friended' on Facebook, but research on the nature of friendship in the USA concludes that Americans say they have few real friends. Miller observes that critics of Facebook suggest that 'friending' represents a 'kind of inflation' of superficial and weak relationships that diminishes the value of true friendship. It is argued that the quality of Facebook relationships can feel inauthentic because they lack the intimacy, vulnerability and physical closeness that characterise real relationships. Gardner and Davis argue that 'friends' may be connected but they may not always be connecting.

Knowledge check 15

What does the phrase 'friends may be connected but they may not always be connecting' mean?

4 It is suggested that social networking sites may cause alienation and loneliness because they create the impression that other people have more friends and are therefore having more fun. Moreover, looking at other people's achievements may make young people feel inadequate and even encourage them to 'stage' happiness and success. Kross and Verduyn found that frequent use of Facebook leads to people becoming less satisfied with life.
5 Digital technology can diminish the quality of face-to-face interaction if people are always focused on their phone and constantly checking for texts and social network updates. Turkle points out that although digital forms of communication connect users to more people, this has also resulted in greater anxiety. She notes devotion to checking the mobile phone is almost religious. When mobile phones are misplaced, anxiety levels rise. People feel cut off from reality. Turkle argues that this is unhealthy behaviour.
6 Digital technology is disruptive because it may reduce family time and closeness. Turkle has argued that the proto-communities of social networking sites and online fantasy gaming such as Second Life are increasingly replacing real communities composed of family, extended kin and neighbours. As a result, the '**post-familial**' family in which family members spend more time interacting with their gadgets than with each other is becoming the norm. Livingstone (2009) in a similar analysis argues that children today communicate more with the virtual outside world than with adult members of their own family. Parents often have to text or Facebook their children to gain their attention at meal times.
7 It is argued that digital media have had a coarsening effect on young people. In particular, it is suggested that they have had the effect of making young people less empathetic and therefore 'meaner' online than they are in person. Online bullying, sexting, grooming and sexual harassment are now recognised as problems of the digital age. Other studies have documented the emotional effects of easy online access to pornography and have expressed fears that adolescent boys' attitudes towards sexual relationships are consequently being shaped by deviant and unrepresentative sexual role models. All of these issues are difficult for sociologists to investigate and for the authorities to police.
8 Despite greater connectivity, some groups are still unable to access or participate in social media.

Post-familial The post-familial family is a family that interacts and communicates via social media and other digital devices rather than face-to-face.

The impact of digital forms of communication on culture

Conflict and change

Castells argues that in the digital age many people have moved away from expressing their political and social concerns through hierarchical and bureaucratic organisations such as governments, political parties, pressure groups, trade unions, religions and so on. The easy availability of digital forms of communication now means that people can organise themselves into non-hierarchical and non-bureaucratic digital networks of like-minded individuals who can mutually share information on the web and organise collective action.

Exam tip

Don't forget to include the concept of cultural homogenisation when you discuss the impact of digital forms of communication on culture.

Castells argues that this **civil society** approach is now an alternative source of political power that is challenging the power of both the state and the market. For example, successful petitioning of those in power has been carried out through Facebook, Twitter and sites such as Change.org. Itzoe observes that the internet and social media have been extensively used by the anti-globalisation movement (also known as the global justice movement) to successfully organise large worldwide protests against global organisations such as the World Trade Organization and the International Monetary Fund, which are seen as partly responsible for global inequality and injustice. Murthy claims that Twitter has the potential to shape many aspects of people's social, political and economic lives. For example, it has proved extremely useful in terms of communicating information about social protest movements such as the Occupy protests in London and New York in 2011, while websites such as WikiLeaks have challenged the power of both the state and large corporations by publishing leaked documents alleging government and corporate misconduct. Digital activists such as the hacker group Anonymous have also engaged in cyberattacks on government and corporate websites.

Civil society Refers to the community of ordinary citizens who are linked by common interests and collective actions. It is argued that civil society is increasingly challenging traditional sources of power such as states and corporations.

There is also evidence that global communication systems and social networks can assist local cultures to rid themselves of repressive political systems such as dictatorships. Both Castells and Kassim argue that the so-called Arab Spring movement that occurred between 2010 and 2013 succeeded in removing totalitarian dictators in Tunisia and Egypt because of global social networks. For example, Facebook was used in Egypt to schedule public protests, Twitter to coordinate, and YouTube to show the world how the authorities had reacted. Kassim argues that these global networks helped Arab people in Egypt and Tunisia to overcome their fears and to take to the streets.

However, critics argue that the role of social media in the Arab Spring has been grossly exaggerated. Curran argues that the Arab Spring was caused by deep-seated economic, political and religious factors, while Wilson and Dunn found that face-to-face interaction, television and print media were more important than social media in getting people onto the streets. Curran concludes that social media played a role in the build-up of dissent and the coordination of protests but they did not cause the uprisings — they merely facilitated them (along with other forms of traditional media).

Knowledge check 16

Identify one argument for and one argument against the idea that digital technology played a big role in the Arab Spring.

Moreover, ideas about the ability of digital communication networks to construct an alternative civil society that can bring about real social change are undermined by the global divide in access to and participation in digital networks. For example, in 2015 the UN announced that 4 billion people — 57% of the world's population and 90% of those who live in the 48 poorest countries — have no access to the internet.

Furthermore, critics argue that it is a fact that states and digital corporations continue to exercise much greater power than digitalised civil society groups. There is a growing tendency in the digital corporate world for power to be concentrated in fewer and fewer more powerful hands. Martell argues that digital technology therefore gives a false impression of more power being given to a greater number of people. He suggests that digital technology may be only a quantitative rather than a qualitative improvement since political information could be obtained before the internet, albeit more awkwardly and slowly. Martell concludes that technologically the internet is revolutionary but it does not necessarily follow that it will have a revolutionary impact on cultural or political life.

Keen is also critical of the idea that the internet and digital technology have the power to politically change the world. He argues that the internet is too chaotically organised to be effective in bringing about change. Moreover, he argues that social networking sites such as Facebook and blogging do not contribute to the democratic process in any way because they are merely vehicles for shameless self-promotion. He further argues that the content of Twitter and blogs often goes unchecked and, consequently, uninformed opinion, lies and trolling are the norm, rather than considered political analysis and expertise. Hader too argues that the power of Twitter to change the world is grossly exaggerated when he described Twitter users as ineffectual and pseudo laptop and iPad revolutionaries.

Cultural defence

Cultural defence Refers to the ways societies attempt to protect their local cultures from globalised culture and the way digital forms of communication are used to support and enhance local culture.

There are a number of ways in which societies and cultures have attempted to protect their domestic media and cultural industries:

- Some countries, for example France, protect their domestic media and cultural industries against the cultural homogenisation brought about by globalisation.
- Some countries have taken control of their digital media. For example, China has blocked all references to the word 'democracy' on its most popular search engine and denies its citizens access to websites such as Wikipedia. All internet use is closely monitored by the authorities. This censorship and surveillance is referred to as the 'great firewall of China'.
- The Muslim world has developed internet websites, political blogs and satellite television channels such as Al-Jazeera to provide an alternative interpretation of what is going on in the Arab world and elsewhere, thereby resisting and opposing Western interpretations.
- In Africa, the expansion of mobile phone technology has had a number of positive effects for local cultures and economies. Greater access to smartphones and social networks has empowered young people to organise themselves online and demand better leadership of their societies. Moreover, there is evidence that mobile phones have had a significant effect on African economies by connecting young consumers over vast distances. Culture too has been enhanced by digital technology. Literacy rates are improving because young people have access to e-books and digital libraries. Healthcare has been improved because it is now possible to access internet medical service providers.
- There is evidence that social networking sites such as Facebook are being used by migrant populations to facilitate connections with their homeland. These connections help them to preserve and defend aspects of their culture, especially language, customs, traditions and religious rites. McKay found when examining the digital experience of Filipinos living and working in London that they used social networking sites to insulate themselves from the individualism that they claimed dominated Western culture. Social networking with relatives and friends in the Philippines meant they could digitally return to the comfort of the types of cultural relationships that they had physically left behind — relationships characterised by obligations to the extended family and ancestors, involvement in the local community from which they had originated, and religious traditions.

- Culturalsurvival.org documents the diverse range of ways in which indigenous tribes and isolated communities are starting to use digital technology to gain a voice that can help defend their cultures from exploitation by corporate interests and other threats.
- However, ISIS is also utilising social media in a very sophisticated fashion — to defend and disseminate its version of Islam. Since 2014 ISIS has posted (mainly on Twitter) photos and statements to highlight details of its operations, including the number of bombings, suicide missions, beheadings and assassinations it has carried out. The group also produces professional promotional videos and urges support for its 'one billion campaign', which calls on Muslims to post messages, photos and videos on Twitter, Instagram and YouTube in support of ISIS. In April 2014, the group even developed a free internet application called The Dawn of Glad Tidings, which automatically posts tweets — approved by ISIS media managers — to the accounts of the application's subscribed users.

Glocalisation

Martell observes that glocalisation has two elements to it. First, Western media and cultural producers often adapt their products so that they appeal to local markets and audiences. For example, MTV adapts its programming according to the cultural likes and dislikes of particular countries such as Japan, India, Mexico, Spain, France and so on and mixes Western music with that produced locally.

Second, local cultures select and appropriate elements of Westernised global culture that please them and which they modify and adapt to local culture and needs. In other words, they 'localise the global' to produce a hybridised popular culture. A good example of this is the Indian film industry — Bollywood combines contemporary Western ideas about entertainment with traditional Hindu myth, history and culture.

Knowledge check 17

Why is Bollywood a good example of a hybridised global culture?

Another good example is Facebook. Miller argues that there is no such thing as Facebook from the perspective of cultural relativity. Facebook is only the aggregate of its regional usage; for example, Facebook in Trinidad is not Facebook in London because two very different cultures, Trinidadian and British, use Facebook in very different ways which reflect their cultural priorities. Miller's research on Facebook use in Trinidad reflects aspects of Trinidadian culture. He observes that locals refer to it as 'Fasbook' or 'Macobook'. These terms are not accidental — they deliberately mirror the cultural inclinations of Trinidadian society, especially the characteristics 'to be fas' (to try and get to know another person rather too quickly) and 'maco' (to be nosy and wanting to constantly pry into other people's business). So activity on Fasbook in Trinidad is mainly geared to getting to know somebody of the opposite sex but once people become friends with one another, they constantly meddle in one another's lives. Fasbook, then, is a good example of **glocalisation** because it has taken the Western idea of a digital communications network but Trinidadians' use of it reflects their local culture.

Glocalisation Refers to how local cultural products are combined or fused with globalised cultural products to produce unique cultural forms or hybrids. It can also refer to how local cultures adapt and use global social networks in ways that reflect the cultural priorities and eccentricities of a particular society.

Held argues that this flow of digital culture is not just one way. Western culture has also been enriched by inputs from the popular culture of other societies. For example, many Western musicians such as Damon Albarn and Robert Plant have worked with African and Arab musicians to fuse genres of music into new forms. Some world music fuses and mixes Western dance beats with traditional styles from North Africa and Asia.

Summary

- Not everybody enjoys equal access to digital forms of communication. Research indicates that a digital divide exists with regard to access to the internet. A digital underclass exists which is denied a digital voice.
- People use social networking sites such as Facebook and virtual worlds to package, promote and present their identities for public consumption, although some sociologists argue that young people's use of digital communication has created a set of modern-day problems for them.
- There is a debate about whether social networking sites are good for society and individuals. Some sociologists argue that they facilitate human interaction, relationships and social capital by constructing a participatory culture. Others have expressed concern that these sites have created a culture of alienation and loneliness which has diminished the quality of human relationships.
- Digital media can act as a resource that helps bring about social change. They have also been used to defend and enhance existing cultural practices.

Section B Crime and deviance

How are crime and deviance defined and measured?

Definitions

- **Crime** refers to activities that break the law of a particular country. They are illegal activities.
- **Deviance** is behaviour that is different from the normal expectations of a society and which is usually viewed as 'wrong' or 'bad'. All crime is deviance but not all deviance is illegal — for example, swearing in the classroom is not illegal but it is regarded as deviant as it is likely to be met with disapproval by teachers.
- **Social order** is the state of social stability and social solidarity that characterises most modern societies. It derives from the fact that citizens generally agree on and therefore share similar values, morals and norms and consequently are reasonably well integrated into society, that is, they share a similar sense of belonging to society. It is maintained by agencies of social control.
- **Social control** refers to the need to regulate the behaviour of citizens of a society in order to make sure they conform to laws and rules so that social order is not threatened. There are two types of social control.
  - **Formal social control** refers to the law. Consequently the function of formal agencies of social control such as the police, courts and prisons is to control, suppress and punish illegal or criminal behaviour. Formal social controls can also comprise organisational rules or regulations.
  - **Informal social controls** are usually aimed at enforcing the sorts of behaviour that society expects of particular individuals. For example, there are social expectations about children's behaviour. If children behave badly and embarrass their parents, they may be informally punished — for example, they may have privileges taken away from them. Peer groups are also informal agencies of social control — for example, friends expect a certain standard of behaviour from one another and failure to live up to that standard may result in a person being excluded from a friendship network.

The relativity of crime and deviance

Sociologists believe that 'normality' and 'deviance' are relative concepts because there is no universal or fixed agreement on how to define them. What is 'normal' behaviour for one social group might be 'deviant' behaviour for another. The notion of relativity can be illustrated in a number of ways.

- First, what counts as deviance depends on the social context in which the activity is carried out. For example, nudity is fine in some circumstances (in the privacy of the bathroom or bedroom and in public places such as nudist camps or particular beaches), is tolerated and regarded as humorous at sporting events (streaking), but is seen as a symptom of mental illness or criminality if persistently carried out in public (i.e. indecent exposure).
- Second, what counts as crime and deviance changes according to historical period, for example homosexuality and attempted suicide were crimes in the UK only 50 years ago.

- Third, definitions of crime and deviance depend on the cultural or subcultural context. For example, drinking alcohol is illegal in Saudi Arabia and disapproved of by Muslims in the UK. What is 'normal' behaviour for a teenager in a particular youth subculture in the UK might be seen as 'deviant' by adult society.

The social construction of crime and deviance

Crime and deviance are the product of cultural expectations and social processes rather than, say, inherent badness or evil. This is because societies make laws or have social expectations in order to control behaviours but these do not remain fixed over time and often differ across societies and within them. For example, soft drug use is socially constructed as criminal by the existence of laws banning their use. However, many young people may interpret the law as old-fashioned and consequently ignore it. There is also evidence that different police forces enforce this law with discretion. Some take it very seriously; others turn a blind eye to it.

Exam tip

The examiner is likely to ask you how 'useful' crime statistics are in measuring crime. A lot of students make the mistake of disproportionately focusing on the weaknesses of these statistics. It is also important to focus on their strengths.

Measuring crime

The official crime statistics

The official crime statistics (OCS), which are published every 6 months by the government, are made up of two types of data:

1. The police record crimes reported by victims, the general public and their own officers.
2. An annual survey — the Crime Survey of England and Wales (CSEW) — of 40,000 people collects data about their experience of crime as victims during the previous year. Supporters of this survey suggest that it is more 'valid' than the police statistics because it includes crimes which have not been reported to the police or not recorded by them for various reasons.

Social construction of statistics Statistics do not occur naturally. They are constructed by human beings making particular social choices and decisions. For example, the choice might be made to target particular behaviour, therefore generating lots of statistics, or to ignore other types of behaviour altogether, therefore generating no statistics.

Some positivist sociologists find the police-recorded crime figures useful in identifying trends and patterns in criminal activity, especially with regard to:

- the volume of crime
- types of crime committed
- the social characteristics of criminals
- the effectiveness of laws and anti-crime policies

However, interpretivist sociologists question the reliability and validity of the OCS. They suggest that police-recorded **statistics** in particular are a **social construction**. They are a product of society rather than objective facts. This is because they only show crimes that are reported to and recorded by the police. In this sense, the OCS may not reflect the reality of crime. Rather they may tell us more about the groups involved in their collection — victims, the general public and the police — than they tell us about crimes and criminals. This can be illustrated in a number of ways:

- Interpretivists point out that the OCS do not account for all the crime committed in the UK. They account only for those crimes that are recognised as such by victims and by the police. Sociologists have long argued that there exists a dark figure of unrecorded crime. For example, criminal offences such as tax and VAT fraud or health and safety infringements are not included in the OCS. Some institutions, for example banks or private schools, may not report crimes because

Exam tip

An alternative way of illustrating hidden crime is by using an iceberg analogy — only the tip of the iceberg (recorded crime) can be seen above the waves. The bulk of the iceberg (unreported and unrecorded crime) lies beneath.

of the bad publicity that may be generated for their institutions. Fee-paying schools may expel or suspend students for criminal activity such as vandalism and drugs, rather than involve the police.

- Victims of crime may not report crime to the police for several reasons:
  - They may regard the crime as too trivial.
  - The perpetrator may be someone they love (for example, wives may not report their husbands for domestic violence).
  - They may regard the crime as too embarrassing (for example, victims of sexual crime may be reluctant to come forward for this reason).
  - They may be too frightened because they fear reprisals.
  - They may not know or realise that a crime has been committed against them (for example, elderly victims of fraud or children who are victims of abuse) or they may mistrust the police.
- In contrast, people are more likely to report crime if they can see the benefit (for example, a police report may be necessary to put in an insurance claim) or if they believe the police are likely to catch the offender. In recent years, the police figures have been distorted by police investigations into historical sexual abuse, that is, offences that have been committed by high-status individuals such as Jimmy Savile decades ago. If a celebrity is found guilty of hundreds of these past offences, they go into the police figures in the year that the guilt is established. This gives the impression that such offences are increasing but in reality this is a statistical illusion.
- Some crimes, for example drug use and prostitution, have no clear victims (they are referred to as **victimless crimes**) and are therefore dependent on police detection. However, there is no national consistency in the policing of these offences.
- It was estimated in 2014 that the police fail to record one in five crimes reported to them. It is argued that they exercise this discretion in recording crime because of the political pressures on them to improve their clear-up rates and to improve their efficiency. These pressures may result in police forces either reclassifying particular crimes as 'less serious' or regarding them as too trivial to record.
- The actual process of policing on the streets may be problematic for the police-recorded figures for three broad reasons.
  - First, the police may exhibit conscious or unconscious bias with regard to the social status of those who report crime. For example, they may not take victims from particular social backgrounds seriously, as exemplified by Owen Gill's study of a working-class community living in Luke Street in Liverpool which suggested that poorer victims of crime were treated more negatively by the police. Black communities have also long complained that the police do not take racist crimes against them seriously.
  - Second, there is evidence that the police stereotype particular social groups — young people, black people, working-class people and people living in particular neighbourhoods — as more 'suspicious' and potentially more criminal, which makes them more likely to stop, search and arrest members of these groups. This suggests that certain groups appear more frequently in the statistics because the police pay them more attention. In contrast, the police are less likely to label middle-class people, women and older people as potentially criminal. They are not paid the same attention and consequently do not turn up in the police statistics very often.

Victimless crimes Usually involve two crimes. A person who sells drugs is committing a crime but so too is the person who buys and consumes them.

Exam tip

It is well worth having some detailed knowledge of the police's treatment of a particular group such as black people to illustrate this important critique of police statistics.

    - Third, police discretion also influences the recorded figures in that if a person or group is stopped, their chances of becoming a police statistic may depend on how the officer interprets their appearance, attitude and manner. Anderson et al. (1994) found that officers were more likely to arrest youth who they interpreted as disrespectful.
- The police-recorded figures are dependent on how the government decides to count crimes and what they decide should be law. For example, the counting rules for crime were extensively changed in 2001–02 especially with regard to violent crime, which, unsurprisingly, increased thereafter. Moreover, between 1997 and 2010 the Labour government introduced 3000 new laws (and therefore new crimes). Any rise or fall in the levels of crime may simply reflect changes in the law as much as actual changes in crime.

  The way the police count crime is based on rules set out by the Home Office. These have changed on a number of occasions, making it difficult to compare like with like over time.

Interpretivist sociologists conclude that all these pressures and influences on the reporting and recording of crime mean that the statistics do not help us in terms of working out how much crime there really is. This can be illustrated by the fact that for every 100 crimes committed, it is estimated that only 47 are *reported to* the police, even fewer, 27, are *recorded by* the police, and only 5 are *cleared up* in the form of a caution or conviction.

Knowledge check 18

Why can't sociologists trust the official crime statistics on sex crimes?

Victim surveys

A second way of estimating the extent and patterns of crime is by using victimisation (or victim) surveys. In these, a sample of the population, either locally or nationally, is asked which offences have been committed against them over a certain period of time. The best known victimisation study is the government's Crime Survey for England and Wales (CSEW), the results of which are now published as part of the OCS. Hoyle observes that these surveys offer a more accurate picture of victimisation than police records supply, and identify the social, economic and demographic characteristics of victims. In the UK, the CSEW has produced a number of interesting findings about the distribution of victims among social groups and the relationship between victims and offenders.

The CSEW has consistently found that young males, especially the unemployed and low-waged, have a particularly high chance of being victims of violence, although most of this involves little or no injury. The older a person gets, the less likely they are to be a victim of crime. Ethnic minorities also report more victimisation than white people. The CSEW has also reported that women are less likely to be victims of crime than men but worry more about crime. Finally, the CSEW data show that there is more crime than is reported to the police (although this gap is narrowing) but a lot of it is fairly trivial in nature.

Realist sociologists such as Lea and Young have been critical of the government's application of victim surveys because the CSEW does not provide detailed information about particular places, and is largely quantitative rather than qualitative. Lea and Young carried out the Islington Crime Survey (ICS) in 1986, which asked victims living in inner-city London about serious crime such as sexual assault, domestic violence and racial attacks in a more in-depth way. This survey found that a third of households in poorer neighbourhoods had been affected by serious crime and women, in particular, had realistic fears about being the victims of sexual crime. Other realist crime surveys suggest that the poor are often the subjects of **repeat victimisation**. This is because: they cannot afford to invest in securing their property; crime disproportionately affects the poor as they often do not have insurance; and they feel that the police are unsympathetic to their plight. Realist victim surveys therefore conclude that poverty is the main variable which makes a person more at risk of being a victim of crime in the UK.

Repeat victimisation Refers to the fact that in deprived inner-city areas being a victim of crime is not uncommon. People can expect to be the victims of burglary or street robbery more than once a year.

However, all types of victim surveys can be criticised for being partial, selective and potentially biased. For example, the CSEW survey excludes certain types of crime such as crimes against businesses and fraud. Homeless people tend to be excluded from most victim survey samples. Such surveys often rely too heavily on the memory of victims despite the fact that the trauma of crime may mean that memories are faulty and biased. Moreover, if a person is unaware that they are a victim of crime, they cannot report it. Finally, despite victim surveys being anonymous, people also tend to under-report being victims of sexual offences.

Knowledge check 19

Suggest two examples of crimes that people may not report because they may be unaware they are victims.

Self-report studies

A self-report is a type of questionnaire which, when used in the sociological study of crime, lists a number of petty criminal acts and asks respondents to tick those they have successfully committed without being caught. Anonymity and confidentiality are usually guaranteed.

Studies based on self-reports, for example Belson on adolescent boys in London and Campbell on teenage girls, indicate that the majority of respondents admit to some kind of illegal activity, which confirms the dark figure of unreported and unrecorded crime. Self-reports indicate that females and middle-class males are just as likely to commit crime. In particular, they have challenged the idea that females commit significantly less crime than males. Campbell found that the ratio of male crime to female crime is 1.5:1 rather than the 7:1 portrayed in the OCS. These self-reports therefore challenge the picture of the typical criminal as male and working class.

The 2003 Offending, Crime and Justice survey, which used self-reports, found that 40% of whites admitted offences compared with just 28% of blacks and 21% of Asians. In contrast, a self-report survey conducted by Sharp and Budd (2005) found that people from mixed-race backgrounds were most likely to admit soft drug use, while 6% of whites admitted using heroin and cocaine compared with only 2% of black people and 1% of Asians.

However, Marsh observes that the self-report method may be unreliable because, despite guarantees of confidentiality and anonymity, some respondents may still not admit committing criminal offences. Research by Junger-Tas (1989) suggests that boys who have had more contact with the criminal justice system were less likely to cooperate with such surveys. Self-report data may not be **representative** because self-reports tend to focus on asking questions about committing petty offences rather than serious crimes. Moreover, the samples of young people used in self-report studies are often unrepresentative in the sense that such questionnaires are often distributed in schools and colleges and may miss school dropouts and truants.

Representativeness Refers to how typical the sample used in a survey is of the general population. It is important to generate representative samples because the researcher can then generalise that what is true of the sample is probably true of everyone else like them.

The validity of the data generated by self-reports may be undermined by under-reporting. People may under-report because self-report studies are retrospective and depend on respondents being able to remember what crimes they have committed in the previous 12 months. However, validity may be undermined by over-reporting too. Boys may exaggerate or over-report their offences to create an impression of 'being tough' or alternatively conceal their crimes because they fear the police might be informed. Attempts that have been made to check the 'honesty' of respondents have indicated that about a quarter of respondents are liable to conceal wrongdoings.

Summary

- There are three main ways of collecting data about crime, who commits it and which groups are more likely to be victims of it: police statistics, victim surveys and self-report surveys.
- The official statistics collected by the police give sociologists useful data in terms of crime trends and types of crime committed. For example, sociologists can say with confidence that property crime has fallen over the last 20 years.
- However, police statistics are also regarded as problematic because some victims, particularly of sex crimes, are still reluctant to report the offence to the police. The police too may be guilty of socially constructing crime statistics by choosing to target particular groups, for example young black men, while ignoring others, for example white-collar criminals.
- The Crime Survey of England and Wales and other victim and self-report surveys are useful tools for giving insight into less serious types of crime but ethical concerns prevent them from fully exploring sexual and violent crime.

What are the patterns and trends in crime?

The social distribution of offending and victimisation

An examination of the official criminal statistics as well as statistics relating to convictions in the courts and the prison population suggests that some social groups are more likely to be arrested, convicted and punished for crime.

Social class

Statistical evidence is not routinely collected by the government on the social-class background of offenders in the UK. However, Robert Reiner observes that there is a working-class bias in the prison population because, prior to being imprisoned, 74% of prisoners were either unemployed or employed in low-paid unskilled manual jobs. Houchin found a strong relationship between living in the most deprived areas of Scotland and being in prison, while Omolade found that 43% of adult prisoners had no academic qualifications and that 60% were on benefits at the time of their conviction. Hagell and Newburn's study of youth detention centres found that only 8% of persistent offenders came from middle-class backgrounds.

Offences can also be differentiated by social class. Middle-class offenders tend to be associated with **white-collar crime**, fraud and tax evasion; working-class offenders are found guilty mainly of burglary and street crime. **Corporate crimes** are most likely to be committed by upper-middle-class corporate professionals and executives, while **state crime** is committed by those in senior positions in government.

White-collar crime Crimes committed by high-status individuals for personal gain (e.g. fraud).

Corporate crime Crimes committed by high-status individuals on behalf of their company (e.g. illegally and cheaply dumping toxic waste to enhance profit and share price).

State crime Crimes, such as acts of genocide or torture defined by international treaties and courts as crimes, committed by agents of the state (e.g. politicians, police officers, members of the armed services).

Some sociologists have suggested that there is class bias in the process of policing and criminalisation. Self-report studies suggest there is little difference in offending between working-class and middle-class young people, so it may be that working-class people, especially the young, are more likely to be negatively stereotyped by the police and courts as potentially criminal, and to be stopped, arrested, prosecuted and sent to prison than other social-class groups. Working-class areas too may be stereotyped and consequently experience greater levels of policing.

However, class differentials in criminalisation may also have something to do with the visibility of crimes committed by different social-class groups. Working-class people are more likely to commit street crimes. Most police resources are focused on the streets, so such crime is likely to be visible to them. In contrast, white-collar, corporate, state and **green crimes** are often complex and invisible to both the general public (who may not even realise that they are the victims of such crime) and the police, who dedicate few resources to policing these types of crime, perhaps because they erroneously underestimate their impact on society.

Green crimes These tend to be a type of corporate crime that damages the environment — for example, a company might dump waste into a river and kill the fish or pollute a clean water supply.

Findings from the CSEW suggest that the risks of being a victim of burglary or theft positively correlate with the level of unemployment in the victim's community. High crime areas tend to be those in inner cities and deprived neighbourhoods, populated by the working class. The risks of being a victim of violent crime are also inversely linked to income — the lower your income, the higher your risk of violent victimisation. Additionally, Kinsey found in the Merseyside Crime Survey in 1984 that the poor suffer more than the wealthy from the effects of crime. For example, a victim of burglary who is uninsured will be hit harder economically than a middle-class victim who has contents insurance. The poor are also more likely to be vulnerable to a range of victimisation — or 'multiple victimisation', according to Young — due to their vulnerable situation and the social problems they face.

Gender

A disproportionally large number of offences are committed by males. Ministry of Justice statistics in 2014 show that men are three times more likely to be taken to court and to be convicted of offences than women, are five times more likely to be arrested, eleven times more likely to be sent to prison and nineteen times more likely to be in prison than females. At least one-third of all men are likely to have been convicted for a criminal offence, compared with only 8% of all women.

Official statistics suggest that women are less likely to be convicted than men for crimes in every offence group. However, when females do commit crime, it is likely to be in the fields of theft (especially shoplifting), fraud and handling stolen goods. There is some evidence that female convictions for violence against the person is rising slowly, although violence is still overwhelmingly a male offence. In 2014 there were 3,826 women in prison in England and Wales compared with about 80,400 men.

Knowledge check 20

Why do you think shoplifting is such a feminine offence?

Self-report data on crimes committed by males and females is mixed. For example, Campbell found that her female sample admitted almost as much crime as her male sample back in the 1980s but fairly recent research by Roe and Ashe suggests that males admit to being more frequent offenders.

Some criminologists argue that these statistics give a false picture of crime as women are more likely to escape detection because police officers do not label women as potential criminals. Some sociologists argue in favour of the **chivalry thesis** — this is the idea that officials in the criminal justice system (from police to judges), who are mainly men, treat women offenders more softly. As a result, females are less likely to be arrested, are more likely to be let off with a warning or caution and, if they do get to the courtroom stage, they are less likely to be convicted or sent to prison if they are found guilty. In the 1990s, Hood found that women were three times less likely to be given prison sentences than men, even for serious offences.

Chivalry thesis Refers to those theories that suggest females do not appear in the criminal statistics as much as males because paternalistic police officers, magistrates and judges treat them more softly or gently than male offenders.

However, feminists are critical of the chivalry thesis. For example, Steward found that women are more likely to be remanded in custody than men, even for trivial offences, while Hedderman reports that women's imprisonment rates in the UK have steadily increased since 2000. Heidensohn argues that the UK criminal justice system is characterised by double standards in that girls and women who deviate from traditional stereotypes of femininity are treated more harshly by magistrates and judges compared with young mothers whom the courts are reluctant to send to prison.

The statistical evidence regarding victimisation suggests that women are less likely to be victims of street violence than men — for example, women comprised only 30% of murder victims in 2013, but they were twice as likely to be the victims of domestic violence and seven times as likely to report being victims of sexual assault.

Seven out of ten homicide victims are male, and they are most likely to be killed by a stranger or an acquaintance. However, over half of female homicide victims since 2003 were killed by a husband or partner.

Age

Statistical evidence shows that the older a person gets, the less likely they are to commit a crime. Most crime is committed by those under the age of 40 years. In 2014, only 12% of the total prison population was aged 60 and over.

The number of crimes committed by young people aged 10–17 years has fallen by about a quarter since 2011, although this age group still commits about 12% of all crime (despite making up only 10% of the population).

However, labelling theory argues that official crime statistics may give a misleading impression of crimes committed by the young because they may be disproportionately targeted by the police. Young people, especially if male, black or Asian and working class, may fit police stereotypes about criminality and consequently may be subjected to greater police attention than older people. Young people may also be paid excessive attention by the mass media via **moral panics**, which may put the police under pressure to stop, search, arrest and prosecute them.

Moral panic Refers to a period of public anxiety about a particular group, activity or event and is usually generated by exaggerated and often distorted mass media coverage, particularly that found in tabloid newspapers.

Although older people are more likely to fear crime, evidence suggests that young people are actually more likely to be victims of crime. The vulnerability of elderly victims should be taken into account, but it is also likely that media over-reporting of 'shocking' crimes against the elderly may give a false impression.

Data on victims of crime under the age of 16 have been systematically gathered since January 2009 by the BCS (British Crime Survey) and its successor the CSEW. The CSEW asks children aged 10 to 15 about their experiences of crime as part of their parents' survey. Using this data, in June 2014, 12% of children had been victims of crime. The majority of these crimes (56%) were categorised as violent crimes, and most of the rest were thefts of personal property.

Ethnicity

Official crime statistics show that, in England and Wales, people from some minority ethnic groups are more likely to be arrested for and convicted of crime than the white ethnic majority.

- Black people, especially African-Caribbeans, who make up only 3.1% of the population, are six times more likely to be stopped and searched by the police than any other ethnic group despite the fact that 90% of such stops do not lead to an arrest. They are twice as likely to be convicted of an offence compared with white people and three times more likely to be sent to prison. In 2014, 13% of male prisoners and one-fifth of female prisoners in UK prisons were black or black British.
- Asian ethnic groups are twice as likely to be stopped and searched as whites but are less likely to be arrested or convicted. About 7.4% of the prison population were British Asian in 2014.
- Ministry of Justice statistics in 2014 showed that the number of Muslims in the prison population more than doubled to nearly 12,000 in the previous 10 years. One in seven prisoners (14%) in England and Wales is a Muslim. Some research suggests around one-third of Muslim inmates are from Caribbean or African backgrounds.

Some sociologists have argued that these statistics suggest that the criminal justice system is both **institutionally racist** and **Islamophobic** and consequently the criminal statistics tell us little about ethnic minority crime. There is strong evidence that suggests racial profiling or stereotyping by some police officers may be a crucial element governing their decision to stop and search people from ethnic minority backgrounds. Research studies by Shiner (2012) revealed that Black people are 30 times more likely than white people to be stopped and searched by police in England and Wales. He describes this police behaviour as 'discriminatory', 'abusive' and 'highly intrusive', and claims this racial profiling was an aggravating factor in the 2012 London riots. Newburn (2007) argues police racism means that officers assume that areas with high proportions of minority ethnic residents are more prone to crime and therefore they deliberately target and over-police those areas.

Interviews with police officers have found evidence of racist attitudes held by individual officers which affect decisions about who to stop and how suspects are treated during stops. Bowling (1999) found many white police officers believed that African-Caribbeans and Asians antagonised white people (and police officers) by failing to adapt to 'British culture'. Holdaway (2002) argues that there is substantial evidence of police racism in what he calls the 'canteen culture' of police stations. His observations of white officers found that racist language, jokes and banter were common.

Interviews with ethnic minority youth about their experience of policing conducted by Wilson and Rees (2006) suggest that young Asian and black males view their encounters with the police very negatively and are convinced that police officers routinely discriminate against them on the basis of racial stereotypes.

There are fears, too, that young Muslim males are being targeted by the government through the **Prevent programme**, as well as the police and courts, from a very early age because of official fears about radicalisation and terrorism. Quraishi (2014) observes that the increasing number of Muslims in prison may reflect the fact that they are under more surveillance because they have become a suspect population in the eyes of law-enforcement agencies.

Islamophobia Refers to prejudice and discrimination practised against Muslims.

Institutional racism Refers to often invisible and unconscious racist practices which are embedded in the way that an organisation or institution is organised. For example, if an organisation is overwhelmingly white in origin, it may fail other cultures by failing to engage with them.

The Prevent programme A state-sponsored policy which came into effect in July 2015 and which instructs all schools to monitor pupils for signs of Islamist radicalisation.

Other sociologists suspect that there is institutional racism at the conviction stage of the judicial process. Ball et al. (2011) analysed over 1 million court records and found that black offenders were 44% more likely than white offenders to be given a prison sentence for driving offences, 38% more likely for public order offences or possession of a weapon and 27% more likely for possession of drugs.

There is evidence from victim surveys that those from ethnic minorities have a higher risk of victimisation. The 2014/15 CSEW shows that the risk of being a victim of personal crime was significantly higher for adults from the mixed, black or black British and Chinese or 'other' ethnic groups than for adults from the white ethnic group. In particular, the proportion of victims from the mixed ethnic group is over twice that seen for the white ethnic group and consistently higher in each of the previous 6 years.

Patterns of crime in a global context

Global organised crime

Globalisation refers to the increasing interconnectedness and interdependence of societies around the world. It involves sharing economic products such as consumer goods and cultural products such as music, television and film. Evidence suggests that criminal behaviour has also become globalised.

Globalisation has resulted in a global criminal economy which Castells estimates is worth over £1 trillion a year. This global organised crime network is involved in the following areas:

- Dealing in illicit drugs — estimated to be worth £300–£400 billion annually. The availability and price of drugs in any city in the UK depend on how efficiently global drug-trade gangs can move drugs around the world while avoiding detection.
- Illegal trafficking in human beings, usually for the purpose of prostitution or slavery.
- Financial crimes such as fraud and **money laundering**.
- Cyber- or internet-based crime which includes credit card fraud, identity theft and phishing (e-mails sent by fraudsters claiming to be from a bank and asking for personal banking details) and hacking.
- Smuggling legal goods such as alcohol, tobacco and cars.
- Counterfeiting designer goods.
- Green crimes, which are damaging to the global environment, such as illegally dumping toxic and radioactive waste in developing countries.
- Violent crimes, particularly terrorism.
- War crimes via the illegal trafficking of weapons.

Taylor points out that the globalisation of crime often creates a 'grey' area between legitimate and illegitimate activities. For example, it is now easy for elite groups and transnational corporations to move funds and profits around the world to avoid taxation. This may lead to an overlap between criminal organisations and the powerful wealthy elites who run the legitimate capitalist global economy, as the former invest in 'legitimate' businesses in an attempt to launder profits from crime.

Money laundering Involves 'cleaning dirty money' earned via crime by investing it in legitimate businesses. For example, money may be channelled through a hotel business by exaggerating the number of people who stay there.

Exam tip

Keep your eyes and ears open for contemporary examples of this overlap for use in the exam. For example, in 2015 HSBC had to pay out £28 million to the Swiss authorities because the bank had been found guilty of laundering drug money.

Castells claims that global criminal networks have developed because globalisation means that knowledge as well as goods and people can move quickly, easily and cheaply across national borders. Hobbs and Dunningham observe that drug crime in the UK is now 'glocal' in character, meaning that it is still locally based but it now has global connections.

Global organised crime often originates in relatively weak states in which law enforcement is either corrupt or feeble to feed demand from the wealthy West for criminal commodities such as drugs. Some global criminal networks have developed because of inequalities in the global capitalist economy and the terms of world trade. For example, in South American countries such as Colombia and Bolivia, local farmers prefer to grow illegal crops such as the coca plant, as it brings in more money from the global economy than growing conventional crops. Cocaine, for example, outsells all of Colombia's other exports combined. Poverty in the developing world is also fuelling people trafficking, which involves paying criminal gangs to be smuggled to the West, where people believe they will be better off.

Global organised crime is difficult to police because international laws are ill defined and international criminal justice agencies do not have the global powers to pursue global criminals. Cooperation between international agencies is limited, or hindered by local corruption, conflict between local and international police agencies and also conflict between governments. Radical criminologists point out that many global crimes are committed by powerful people, who use their influence to ensure that no laws exist to criminalise their activities, and that no punishment is likely.

Newburn has identified three consequences of globalisation for crime and criminals:

1 It is almost impossible for individual countries to fight particular types of crime within their borders because the crime originates from outside the country. For example, cyberfraud, which claims UK victims, may emanate from sites in eastern Europe.
2 Globalisation has created new opportunities for crime. For example, the main criminal motive for people trafficking until recently was the profit to be made from forced prostitution and domestic slavery.
3 Countries are now more aware of the global risks brought about by crimes such as terrorism. Beck calls this '**global risk consciousness**'. It refers to the fact that, in the past, any risk of becoming a victim of crime originated in our local environment. Increasingly, however, we are now at risk from crime such as terrorism that originates thousands of miles away.

Green crime

Green crime refers to crime against the environment. Green crime is increasingly seen as a form of global crime, for two reasons:

- The planet is a single ecosystem in which human beings, other species and the environment are interconnected and interdependent.
- The borders of nation-states are not a defence against the effects of green crime. For example, radioactive fallout from the Chernobyl nuclear reactor disaster of 1986 spread thousands of miles across Europe, resulting in the banning of sheep farming in parts of England and Wales.

Knowledge check 21

Why might traditionally local crimes such as burglary, street robbery and shoplifting now be described as 'glocal' crimes?

Global risk consciousness Refers to the fact that populations, especially those living in richer countries, are becoming increasingly aware of the downside of globalisation — for example, terrorism, the spread of viruses such as Ebola and Zika, refugees and economic migrants — and are increasingly opposed to state policies that expose them to these 'risks'.

Sociologists who are interested in green crime usually take one of the following positions:

- They focus only on those green crimes which are illegal, that is, criminalised by local or international laws. For example, some nations might break international agreements regarding fishing or emissions of greenhouse gases.
- Sociologists such as South believe that definitions of environmental harms should be extended to behaviour which is not actually illegal but which has the potential to have negative global effects.

South identifies two broad types of offence he argues should be regarded as green crimes:

1. Primary green crime refers to those activities which are not currently illegal but which nonetheless destroy or seriously degrade the planet's ecosystem or local environments. South includes various types of pollution of air, oceans and clean water supplies, deforestation, as well as exploitation of natural resources that results in species decline in this category.
2. Secondary green crime refers to behaviour which does involve breaking existing laws such as causing industrial pollution and disasters by flouting health and safety laws (as in the Bhopal chemical factory disaster of 1984, which killed at least 4,000 people in India) or dumping toxic waste near human settlements instead of following safe but expensive modes of disposal.

However, White argues that definitions of green crime need to be extended to include the notion of 'harm' to nature rather than just to humans or animal species. He advocates that green sociology needs to be underpinned by '**zemiology**' — the study of social harms, whether they are legal or not.

He is particularly critical of current international laws aimed at protecting the environment because these are 'anthropocentric' — they assume that humanity has the right to exploit the environment and consequently such laws are mainly aimed at protecting humans from the effects of this 'corporate colonisation of nature'. However, corporate greed shapes the law-making process and law-makers rarely consider the long-term risks for either humanity or the planet.

White argues that criminologists need to take an **eco-centric** approach to defining environmental harm because any damage to the planet and its non-human species is likely to have negative consequences for humanity at some future point in time.

Ulrich Beck observes that many of the threats to the environment and, in the long term, life on Earth are the product of what he calls 'manufactured risks'. Beck argues that in pre-modern societies, many of the risks to human life were the products of forces outside people's control. For example, poor people had no control over their poverty and the diseases that resulted from this that killed their children. People were also constantly at risk from natural phenomena such as earthquakes and floods. In modern society, technology and science developed to minimise these risks. Mass food production and modern medicine minimised the risks caused by poverty, while scientists began predicting the risks brought about by natural forces, for example through more accurate weather forecasting, enabling societies to take

Zemiology Originated as a critique of conventional criminology and how crimes are defined. Zemiologists argue that definitions of crime should be extended to include the social and environmental harms committed by corporations and nation-states.

Eco-centric Refers to putting the environment or ecosystem first. White is arguing that damage to our natural environment will eventually damage humanity.

successful action to avoid natural disasters or to minimise their effects. However, in late modernity, Beck claims that massive demand for consumer goods and economic growth have created or **manufactured** new global **risks** such as global warming, climate change, cancers, obesity and exposure to nuclear radiation, chemicals and gases to which we are all, regardless of whether we live in the developed or developing world and regardless of social class, equally vulnerable.

However, regardless of how green crime is defined, it has proved difficult to police and punish for two main reasons:

- There are few local or international laws governing the state of the environment. Current laws are inconsistent because they often differ across different countries. France's environmental laws, for example, may not focus on the same harms as the environmental laws that exist in the UK.
- Many of the environmental laws that do exist are influenced by powerful transnational oil, mineral and chemical companies and are constructed in ways that do not threaten their operations or profits. Politicians, especially in the developing world, are reluctant to legislate against transnational corporations because these companies are economically powerful.

Manufactured
Manufactured risks are those which emanate from the science and technology involved in the manufacture and use of consumer goods. For example, in 2015, it was observed that 29,000 people at least die from the effects of air pollution in the UK.

Knowledge check 22

Why are transnational companies rarely policed?

Summary

- A superficial examination of statistics suggests that sociologists can construct social profiles of criminality. For example, most criminals come from poorer socioeconomic backgrounds, most are young men and, in some areas, they are disproportionately black or Asian.
- However, more critical analysis suggests that the notion that some groups are more criminal than others is undermined when the social construction of the statistics is examined.
- There is considerable evidence that policing strategies are over-focused on some groups — young working-class men, African-Caribbeans and recently Muslims — and that the police target their resources in areas where these groups are found. The statistics may therefore tell sociologists more about police priorities, strategies and prejudices than they tell them about crime and criminals.
- In contrast, some groups — women, the middle classes and older generations — may appear less in the statistics not because they are less criminal but simply because the police pay them less attention.
- Globalisation has changed the nature of local crime, while bringing about new risks. For example, crimes such as burglary are often motivated by addiction to a drug grown and processed thousands of miles away, while Islamist terrorism does not recognise national boundaries.
- Green crime is a type of corporate and state crime which is gaining increasing attention as the world's environment is degraded and the future of the planet is increasingly put at risk. However, many green harms are not actually criminal in law and therefore cannot be controlled because those responsible for making laws are often the same governments creating the conditions in which such harms flourish, for example by failing to legislate against powerful industrial and chemical corporations.

How can crime and deviance be explained?

Theoretical views of crime and deviance

Functionalism

Functionalists argue that crime and deviance can only be explained by looking at the way societies are organised socially — their social structures — and that crime is caused by society rather than being the product of evil or the circumstances of the individual. Functionalism is, therefore, a **structuralist theory** of crime.

Structuralist theories Ones that look for the causes of social phenomena such as crime in the way that societies are structured or organised. For example, societies might be organised along social class or patriarchal or tribal lines.

Durkheim

Émile Durkheim believed that, in pre-industrial societies, crime was fairly rare because family and religion were powerful agencies of socialisation and social control. These agencies ensured that individuals conformed to a value consensus which reflected the interests of the whole community. Any deviance from this consensus would be subject to severe punishment, for example exile or death.

However, Durkheim argued that industrialisation resulted in widespread urbanisation and the gradual tolerance of new ways of thinking, especially scientific and rational explanations of how the world worked. Durkheim believed that the complexity of modern industrial life had the effect of undermining the authority of religion and the family. He claimed that, as a result, consensus, community, social controls and punishments were weaker in modern societies, and people were more likely to experience moral uncertainty and confusion — he called this 'anomie' — about how they should behave, therefore increasing the potential for both crime and deviance.

However, Durkheim observed that crime was present in most societies and consequently speculated that it must perform positive functions which benefit society, for example the following:

- Some crimes can provoke positive social change by highlighting aspects of social life or the law that are unjust. For example, the suffragette movement deliberately broke the law in order to highlight gender inequalities in the early twentieth century. The activities of these **functional rebels** eventually resulted in women being given the vote.
- Some crimes such as terrorist attacks or the murder of children create such public outrage that they reinforce and reinvigorate both consensus and community solidarity.
- The pursuit, trial and punishment of wrongdoers function to maintain the boundaries between good citizens and criminals because society is reminded that failure to follow social rules will not be tolerated.

Functional rebel An individual or group that commits criminal or deviant acts in order to bring about a positive outcome such as justice or equality.

However, Durkheim never explained why particular social groups commit crime in the first place or why particular groups who do, get away with it. Critics point out that many crimes are actually dysfunctional, that is, they have negative consequences for both individuals and societies. Marxists also argue that Durkheim over-focused on consensus to the extent that he underestimated the level of conflict and inequality in modern societies, which in itself may be a cause of crime.

Merton

An American functionalist, Robert Merton, argued that the cause of crime lies in the relationship between the culture and the social structure or organisation of society. In capitalist societies, cultural institutions, such as the mass media, socialise individuals into believing that material success is a realistic goal.

Functionalists Davis and Moore argued that many Western societies were meritocratic — this means that they test people's talent, skill and effort via objective examinations and reward success with qualifications, jobs, high salaries and upward social mobility. Davis and Moore argued that such societies were fair because people only got ahead on **merit**.

Merit Ability, skill and hard work — a meritocracy is a society in which people are awarded only on the basis of merit.

However, Merton was critical of the idea that societies such as the USA were meritocratic. He argued that the resources and opportunities provided by the social structure of societies are not fairly distributed because the means of achieving the goal of material success — education and jobs — are not fairly distributed and consequently some social groups experience greater advantages than others. In other words, the playing field was far from level.

Exam tip

Be aware that Merton's theory is sometimes called 'blocked opportunities theory' or 'anomie' theory or 'strain' theory.

Merton therefore argues that the causes of crime in the USA lie in the apparent strain or mismatch between the cultural goals set by powerful ideas such as the American dream (which is transmitted by parents to their children, schools and the mass media) and the legitimate institutional means (education and work) of achieving those goals. The fact that these institutional means are dominated by privileged groups means that many talented members of society have their opportunity to make it to the top blocked.

Knowledge check 23

What is meant by strain theory?

Merton refers to the strain between goals and means as 'anomie' and argues that it results in a large section of a population becoming disillusioned, frustrated, disaffected and potentially criminal. In fact, Merton identifies five possible responses to anomie:

1. **Conformity.** This is the majority response. People continue to strive towards the goal of material success by going to work and therefore conform to the social rules.
2. **Innovation.** Innovators are people who realise that material success is unlikely to be achieved through legitimate means such as going to work every day. They therefore choose to adopt illegitimate means, that is, criminal means, in order to achieve the American dream. For example, American gangsters such as Lucky Luciano and Al Capone are good examples of innovators. Merton observes that gangsters are not that different to law-abiding citizens. They share the same cultural goal pushed by cultural agencies such as the media — to achieve material success.
3. **Ritualism.** Ritualists are people who have given up on the goal of material success but seek solace and satisfaction by immersing themselves in their jobs.
4. **Retreatism.** Retreatists have abandoned both conventional goals and means and retreated from mainstream society altogether by becoming dependent on drugs or drink, by deliberately becoming homeless or by committing suicide.

5 **Rebellion.** Rebels reject the mainstream goal of material success and the normal means of achieving this because they believe such goals and means to be politically or morally wrong. Rebels usually want to tear down the existing system, often through violent revolution or the use of terror tactics, and replace it with their own.

Merton's theory was very influential and has influenced other important theories such as Cohen's theory of juvenile delinquency and Cashmore's theory of why black youth commit crime. Sumner claims that Merton has uncovered the main cause of crime in modern societies — the alienation caused by disillusion with the impossible goals set by capitalism.

However, there are several criticisms of Merton.

- He does not explain why some individuals innovate by committing crime, yet others conform, retreat or rebel.
- He explains crime that results in economic gain because he sees this as originating in the dominant cultural goal of material success. However, many types of crime, especially violent and sexual crimes, are not motivated by money.
- He fails to explain crimes committed by young people in **gangs**, who are more likely to be motivated by a search for excitement or peer pressure or status rather than material goals.
- He only explains crimes committed by poorer sections of society. His explanation of blocked opportunities fails to explain white-collar, corporate and state crimes.

Gangs A type of deviant and/or criminal subculture in which peer pressure shapes behaviour.

Merton fails to ask who benefits from the capitalist system and especially the laws that underpin it.

Marxism

The Marxist analysis of society is focused on how the capitalist economic system generally benefits the capitalist ruling class at the expense of the majority of the population. Marxists also argue that the nature and organisation of capitalism creates the potential for criminal behaviour in all social classes.

This can be illustrated in two ways. First, Gordon argues that the population of capitalist societies is socialised into a set of capitalist values that includes competition, individualism, materialism, conspicuous consumption, selfishness and greed, and that these values are **criminogenic**, meaning that they encourage criminal behaviour among rich and poor alike. He also argues that the profit motive encourages a culture of greed and self-interest. The need to win at all costs or go out of business, as well as the desire for self-enrichment, encourage capitalists to commit white-collar and corporate crimes such as tax evasion.

Criminogenic Refers to anything which is likely to produce crime.

Second, Gordon argues that capitalism is characterised by class inequalities in the distribution of, for example, wealth and income, poverty, unemployment and homelessness. He suggests that most crime committed by poorer sections of society is a realistic and rational response to these inequalities. Capitalism also encourages a 'culture of envy' because poorer sections of society are bombarded with representations of wealth by the mass media and this may also encourage criminality as the alienated poor want what better-off groups take for granted.

Knowledge check 24

Why do Marxists describe crimes committed by the poor as rational?

Althusser (1970) argues that control of the proletariat is maintained through the repressive state apparatus (RSA), which directly and obviously controls the proletariat through violence or the threat of violence, and the ideological state apparatuses (ISAs), which control us more subtly, by socialising us into accepting the capitalist ideology. The RSA comprises the government, the armed forces, the police and the criminal justice system, whereas examples of ISAs include the family, the media, education and religion. Althusser argues that the ISAs are important because no class can hold power over a long period without exercising ideological control, since violent repression breeds resentment and opposition.

The RSA and ISA function in the interests of the capitalist class to maintain and legitimate class inequality in the following ways:

- They are concerned mainly with protecting the major priorities of capitalism — wealth, private property and profit. Snider notes that the capitalist state is reluctant to pass laws that regulate the activities of businesses or threaten their profitability.
- Box notes that the powerful kill, injure, maim and steal from ordinary members of society but these killings, injuries and thefts are often not covered by the law. For example, a worker's death due to employer infringements of health and safety laws is a civil, rather than criminal offence.
- Law enforcement is selective and tends to favour the rich and powerful. In particular, white-collar and corporate crimes are under-policed and under-punished. For example, social security fraud, largely committed by the poor, inevitably attracts prosecution and often prison, yet tax fraudsters, who are usually wealthy and powerful individuals or corporations rather than ordinary taxpayers, rarely get taken to court. Reiman argues that the more likely a crime is to be committed by higher-class people, the less likely it is to be treated as a criminal offence.

Marxists are particularly interested in the white-collar and corporate crimes committed by the powerful. White-collar crime refers to crime committed in the course of legitimate employment, usually by people with power within an organisation, for example managers, accountants etc., who are able to use their occupational role to evade detection. Fraud, accounting offences, tax evasion, insider dealing and computer crime are typical white-collar crimes.

Corporate crime involves high-ranking officials who own or manage companies carrying out illegal or morally suspect activities to enhance the profits of the company. This may indirectly benefit those individuals, in that increased profits will probably result in increased financial rewards for those who run the companies.

These are not minor offences. For example, in 2006–07, 241 workers in the UK were killed in avoidable accidents at work. In the same period, 90 members of the general public also died as a direct result of health and safety infringements. Moreover, the financial costs to society of white-collar and corporate crimes are at least 24 times greater than the cost of working-class street crime, according to Thio.

However, Croall observes that white-collar and corporate crime are rarely reported, detected and prosecuted. Crime is generally seen by the authorities, the media and the general public as a working-class problem rather than a middle-class or upper-class problem. She suggests that this is because crimes of the powerful generally tend to be:

- indirect — offenders and victims rarely come into contact with one another
- largely invisible — people often don't realise they have been a victim of a corporate crime such as price-fixing

- complex — corporate crime often involves the abuse of complex technical, financial or scientific knowledge and is therefore beyond the comprehension of most people
- less feared — because it is invisible, indirect and complex
- morally ambiguous — some crimes, particularly tax evasion, may be admired and tolerated by the general public because nobody likes paying tax

Moreover, Croall observes that it is difficult to decide where the blame lies for corporate crimes. Does it, for example, lie with the Board of Directors or does it lie with individual executives or managers?

Evaluation of Marxist criminology

Traditional Marxist criminology has been criticised for largely ignoring the relationship between crime and important non-class variables such as ethnicity and gender. It sees all laws as representing ruling-class interests and consequently ignores the fact that the law also protects the interests of vulnerable groups such as children, women and ethnic minorities. Marxism also fails to explain why the criminal justice system has successfully prosecuted some powerful individuals and companies.

Neo-Marxist or radical criminology

Neo-Marxists are critical of traditional Marxist ideas on crime, especially the idea that the working class is driven to crime by factors beyond its control such as poverty, inequality or criminogenic values. Neo-Marxists are influenced by **social action theory**, in that they believe that people interpret the world around them and choose to behave in certain ways. Criminality, therefore, is a deliberate choice — it is usually the result of the 'criminal' interpreting their experience of inequality or capitalism and deciding that what they have experienced is 'unjust' or in need of change.

Social action theory Theory focusing on how people choose to interact in groups and how they interpret the meaning of one another's behaviour. It is often contrasted with structuralist theories which see human behaviour as shaped by social forces beyond their control. Social action theory stresses the role of free will and sees societies as socially constructed through interaction and interpretation.

Neo-Marxists such as Taylor, Walton and Young argued that the action that derives from this interpretation is a political action. For example, from this perspective, theft, robbery and burglary are attempts to redistribute wealth from the rich to the poor, vandalism is a symbolic attack on capitalism's obsession with property, while drug addiction reflects contempt for the material values of capitalism.

Neo-Marxists, therefore, argue that criminals are revolutionaries struggling to alter capitalist society for the better. Moreover, they argue that the ruling class is aware of this threat and seeks to contain it by:

- introducing draconian laws to control the potentially troublesome working-class and ethnic minority population
- intensively policing working-class areas so that the police resemble an army of occupation in some areas
- creating moral panics that aim to divide and rule the working class by convincing white working-class people that they have more to fear from immigrants, asylum seekers, Muslims and black crime than they do from those who run society

Evaluation of neo-Marxism

However, neo-Marxism has been criticised because while the political motives for demonstrations, riots, assassinations and terrorism can be seen, it is clearly nonsensical to suggest that crimes against the vulnerable can be explained using political justifications. The neo-Marxist theory also implies that ordinary criminals possess a political consciousness which underpins each decision to commit crime — although this is highly unlikely because most crime is opportunistic.

Interactionism

Interactionism (which incorporates labelling theory) is an interpretivist theory of crime, which means it is interested in how people interpret the world around them and, in particular, how they interact with others.

Interactionists reject the functionalist idea of value consensus, particularly with regard to what counts as normality or deviance. Interactionists observe that these concepts are relative — they mean different things to different people and groups. For example, young people's concept of deviance may be quite different to that of their parents. Furthermore, definitions of normality or deviance often differ according to social context (for example, nudity is fine in private but not on the streets), historical period (for example, homosexuality and boxing were criminal offences in the past) and culture (for example, Muslim culture defines drinking alcohol and gambling as deviant).

Becker claims that deviance is in the eye of the beholder because an act only becomes deviant when it is interpreted by others with more power. Becker claims that deviance is a social construction because it requires the activity of two groups — one group acts in a particular way and another with more power interprets and evaluates that activity as wrong or problematical. This **social reaction** results in the labelling of the activity as illegal and the group as deviant or criminal.

Social reaction Refers to the reaction of others, especially powerful others, who have the influence to define or label behaviour as normal or deviant. Social action theory observes that behaviour is not labelled as deviant until it has provoked a strong negative social reaction from powerful groups such as the mass media, religious leaders, police officers and judges.

Becker argues that powerful groups socially construct deviance and criminality by making rules and laws — the breaking of these leads to the powerful imposing their interpretations of what is normal or deviant on society. At a local level, parents and teachers make rules for young people but at a national or societal level, interactionists believe the economically and politically powerful decide on behalf of society what counts or does not count as criminal behaviour. This social construction of law and therefore crime is sometimes motivated by some sort of social consensus.

As social values and morals evolve, the majority may feel that social change is required (for example, as society grew more liberal, so laws criminalising homosexuality were repealed). However, critical interactionists argue that most laws reflect the interests of the powerful rather than any value consensus. Consequently, harms committed by multinational corporations (for example, harms to consumers, employees and the environment) and states (for example, mass killing) may not be interpreted and hence defined as unlawful. These activities may be deliberately excluded from the law.

Interactionists argue that the powerful often socially construct crime and deviance through other agents such as the mass media, the police and the judiciary.

- The mass media socially construct moral panics which interpret and label the activities of less powerful groups, especially younger people, as deviant or criminal, thereby justifying stricter controls over them, for example in the form of new laws.
- The police socially construct crime and (therefore the official criminal statistics) by interpreting and labelling the activities of groups such as the working class and ethnic minority males as more criminal than other social groups, and then targeting and over-policing those groups.

- Hood found that the courts socially construct crime by interpreting and labelling crime committed by young African-Caribbeans as requiring greater punishment than the same crime committed by young whites.

Interactionism has also focused on the effects or consequences of labelling people as deviants or criminals. Lemert distinguishes between **primary deviance** (deviance that goes unobserved and consequently does not attract the public label of deviant) and secondary deviance (behaviour which results from a societal reaction and which results in a negative label being attached). Lemert argues that secondary deviance is the more important type because it results in very negative consequences for those labelled as deviant or criminal. He argues that a negative label can impose great psychological and social damage on an individual.

Lemert points out that deviant labels often become **master statuses**. This means that when ordinary people interact with people who have been labelled as criminals or deviants the former judge the latter purely on the basis of the negative label rather than on their other statuses such as son, husband, father, friend and so on.

One of the consequences of this negative labelling is that the 'deviant' may be forced to seek the company of others who have been similarly labelled in order to experience normality. This may lead to the development of a subculture of deviance, which increases the chances of a return to deviant ways of behaving.

Interactionists therefore conclude that labelling may result in a **self-fulfilling prophecy**. The labelled person lives up to their master deviant status because they are not trusted by society and their resulting unemployment and poverty motivate more crime. Interactionists also argue that labelling can result in deviancy amplification. The original 'deviance' is amplified as the person labelled deviant reacts to the negative labelling by becoming even more deviant in symbolic protest. For example, there is evidence that some young people in the UK saw ASBOs as a badge of honour which they needed to live up to by getting into more trouble.

The strengths of interactionism

Interactionism has shown that defining deviance is a complex rather than a simple process — that it is socially constructed through interaction with others and that deviance is very often a matter of interpretation. Moreover, it has clearly shown that definitions of deviance are relative and therefore not fixed, universal or unchangeable. Definitions of deviance and crime are constantly in a state of change, as is the law. Interactionism also shows that the law is not applied equally to all social groups. It often enforces selectively, for example some groups are afforded more attention by the police and therefore crime statistics may tell sociologists more about policing than criminality. Finally, interactionism was the first theory to draw attention to the social consequences of being labelled a deviant and, most importantly, to show that society's attempts to control deviance can backfire and create more deviance rather than less.

The weaknesses of interactionism

Akers argues that interactionism puts too much emphasis on societal reaction. Although it is important in some cases, he argues that some criminal acts, for example murder, rape and child abuse, are so dreadful that the act will always be more important than the reaction to it. Also, the notion of social reaction implies that people who commit deviant acts are unaware that they are doing wrong until someone

Primary deviance Refers to acts of deviance that go unnoticed. Perpetrators are therefore not labelled as deviant. In contrast, secondary deviance is linked to how society reacts to those people who are observed committing deviant acts.

Master status The most important characteristic in the collection of statuses that make up a person's identity. If a deviant characteristic is added to the set, for example paedophile or ex-con, this may override all the other statuses a person occupies and shape society's reaction to the individual.

Exam tip

Examiners often ask about subcultures. Be aware that a range of theories focus on these in one way or another.

Self-fulfilling prophecy Refers to the social process whereby a prediction is made about the future behaviour of a person. All interaction with that person is shaped by the predicted label and consequently the person lives up to that label and fulfils the original prophecy.

with more power points it out to them. This might be the case with children but adults do not need to wait until a label is attached to understand that what they are doing is wrong.

Left realists claim that interactionism is guilty of failing to explain why people commit deviant acts in the first place, probably because it is too focused on the societal reaction and the consequences of labelling. There is an unfortunate tendency in interactionism to suggest that the real problem lies with groups such as the media and the police — or indeed to blame anyone but the person labelled as a deviant. Hence interactionists often end up romanticising offenders as victims of the establishment. For example, they claim that the reason young people appear more in the crime statistics is that they are unfairly labelled by the media and police and are therefore unjustly policed and punished. The focus is rarely on *why* some people might be motivated to commit crime or *why* they choose to commit particular types of crime or deviance rather than others. Furthermore, interactionists often neglect the victims of crime.

Marxists argue that although interactionism acknowledges the role of power, it does not explain the origin of that power. Marxists, of course, argue that power originates in class relationships and that labelling is an ideological process which supports the interests of the ruling class and is often used by that class to socially control the powerless.

Knowledge check 25

How does societal reaction towards social security fraud and tax fraud support this Marxist criticism of interactionism?

Left realism

The left **realists** Jock Young and John Lea are 'left' in that they agree with Marxists that capitalism is a deeply unequal system in terms of income, wealth and opportunity, and consequently those social groups at the bottom of the socioeconomic ladder regularly experience the shame and humiliation of living on the breadline. They are 'realists' because their victim survey of London (the Islington Crime Survey) found that most victims reported that most offenders were young working-class white and black men.

Realists Those who believe that crime is not socially constructed by the police or media but instead is a very real problem that blights ordinary people's lives.

However, left realists attempt to explain crime from the point of view of the criminal and suggest that crime comes about because of four very important influences.

1 **Individualisation.** Capitalist societies have become less community orientated because the mass media have encouraged a 'me culture' obsessed with achieving monetary and materialistic goals. Consequently, people now look out for themselves and their immediate family rather than the communities in which they live. This increasing individualism means that community and neighbourhood controls over crime and deviance have weakened.
2 **Relative deprivation.** Capitalist societies are deeply unequal societies in terms of wealth and income. However, the media have also made people aware of how much they have or lack compared with similar groups of people. Left realists argue that those at the very bottom of society (the working class and ethnic minorities) may feel '**relatively deprived**' compared with their middle-class or white peers. They see these peers enjoying material comforts such as designer labels and feel that they should have access to the same. They feel frustrated, angry and hostile because they see their route to these material things as blocked by society.

Relative deprivation Refers to the idea that social groups look at other groups similar to themselves to see what they are missing out on.

3 **Marginalisation.** Left realists argue that feelings of relative deprivation are worsened by feelings of powerlessness. Those at the bottom of society may feel marginalised. This means they feel that they cannot change their situation because they are not represented by powerful interests such as political parties. Moreover, they may also feel that they have been unfairly stigmatised for their poverty by the police (who constantly stop and search them) and the media which dismiss them as lazy and as scroungers. Lea and Young also suggest that these feelings of marginalisation are reinforced by the military-style policing of inner-city areas and procedures such as stop and search. As a result, they note, there is a great deal of pent-up frustration and hostility among inner-city populations that may erupt now and then into riots and looting.
4 **Subcultural responses.** The combination of relative deprivation and marginalisation may express itself in subcultural form as people with similar experiences and frustrations come together. Some of this subcultural response may be expressed through crime as young men, both black and white, get involved in territorial street gangs and attempt to relieve their feelings of deprivation and marginalisation through violence, drug dealing, etc. Subcultural responses may also be retreatist as people become addicted to hard drugs as a means of coping with the boredom and humiliation of poverty. However, some subcultural responses can be positive too. Many of the deprived and marginalised may find compensation in sporting success or comfort in religion.

Exam tip

Note that left realism is yet another theory that sees a central role for subcultures.

Strengths of left realism

Hughes notes that the strength of left realism is that it attempts to describe and explain why most street crime occurs in deprived inner-city areas. Most importantly, it does not attempt to over-romanticise the young working-class white and black males which left realists see as most responsible for this crime. Left realists have also highlighted the effect of crime on victims. They have clearly shown that most victims of crime are members of deprived groups, a fact that most theories of crime have ignored or neglected.

Weaknesses of left realism

There is no empirical evidence to support the view that young working-class or black criminals feel deprived and marginalised and that this is the main motive that underpins their criminal behaviour. Moreover, even if this were the case, left realists do not explain why the majority of working-class and African-Caribbean males living in inner-city areas are law-abiding and never get into trouble with the police. Finally, left realism focuses only on collective or subcultural criminal responses and does not explain crimes such as burglary that are committed by individuals rather than gangs.

New Right and right realism

The New Right sociologists, Charles Murray and David Marsland, argue that most crime in both the USA and the UK is committed by a highly deviant, immoral and workshy subculture called the 'underclass'. This group is allegedly made up of 'problem families' living on inner-city council estates who are dependent on state benefits and who socialise the next generation into seeing criminal and antisocial behaviour as 'normal'.

Exam tip

The underclass is yet another subculture.

However, both Murray and Marsland have been accused of negatively stereotyping and scapegoating the poor. There is no empirical evidence that the underclass subculture actually exists. Surveys of the poor living in deprived areas suggest they generally subscribe to values and aspirations not that dissimilar to the rest of society.

A more sophisticated right-wing theory of crime and deviance is right realism. First, Clarke argues that criminals have free will and choose to commit crime on the basis of a rational weighing-up of the benefits of crime (for example, the financial reward) against the potential costs (for example, the possibility of being caught and punished). Clarke argues that crime has increased for the following reasons:

- Policing is poor. Criminals know there is little chance of being caught.
- Community controls are weak. For example, ordinary people in high crime areas are too afraid to speak out against criminals.
- Punishments are too lenient. For example, offenders are more likely to get community service than prison.

Second, Travis Hirschi suggests that most people do not commit crime because the costs of crime to them as individuals always outweigh the benefits. This theory is also known as control theory. There are four main controls that mean that the costs of crime will always outweigh the benefits for most people:

- **Attachment.** Most people fear losing the love and respect of their partners and family.
- **Commitment.** Most people fear losing their jobs, their homes, their standard of living etc.
- **Involvement.** Most people fear losing their positive reputation and the respect of their friends, colleagues, community etc.
- **Belief.** Most people have been successfully socialised into respecting others, obeying the law etc.

However, both Clarke and Hirschi can be criticised as there is no empirical evidence supporting their claims. Postmodernists such as Katz argue that delinquency is often unplanned, spontaneous and certainly not rational. It is often thoughtless — offenders rarely think about the consequences either for the victim or for themselves. Katz argues that delinquency is motivated by young men's search for thrills, excitement and pleasure. He claims that this search for thrills, or **transgression** as he calls it, is rooted in masculinity and that it aims to counter the boredom of everyday life.

Transgression A deliberate act that goes against a law, rule or code of conduct in order to produce pleasure, thrills and excitement.

The third and very influential version of right realism is the 'broken windows' theory of Wilson and Kelling, which sees the decline of inner-city communities as responsible for the rise in crime. They argue that if a community allows its physical environment to decline — for example, if it does not mend broken windows, clean up graffiti, and move on or arrest antisocial groups of young people or people who deal drugs in public places — criminals and delinquent gangs will assume that local social or community controls no longer exist and see this as an excuse to commit even more crime.

However, the broken windows thesis can be criticised for failing to take on board wider structural reasons for crime such as inequalities in wealth and income, the persistence of poverty and the cultural emphasis that success equals material gain, which potentially create a culture of envy or relative deprivation among society's 'have nots'. It reduces solutions to crime to short-term fixes, for example cleaning up the neighbourhood, rather than long-term economic investment in deprived communities to generate jobs.

Knowledge check 26

How are left and right realism similar and different?

Subcultural theories

Subcultural theories focus mainly on crimes committed by young people in groups or gangs (although other theories such as labelling theory, left realism and the New Right have subcultural elements, too).

Albert Cohen's subcultural theory aimed to explain the emergence of street gangs in the USA in the 1950s but it is still useful today for its insights into why young people organise themselves in this way. Cohen claimed that gangs or subcultures were the product of 'status frustration'. He argued that young people, like any other group, desire status, respect and attention. Most young people achieve these goals via approval from their families or at school. However, working-class young men may be denied status and respect, particularly in education, because their families have failed to equip them with the necessary academic and social skills. Cohen argued that they react to this social slight by forming anti-school subcultures inside school and anti-social street gangs outside school that award status and respect on the basis of acting out deviant values — they earn status from each other by breaking the rules of school and society.

Similar to this is Sutherland's theory of differential association, which argues that if the majority of teenagers in an area are acting in a deviant way, it is difficult for the rest of the group not to be influenced by such behaviour.

Knowledge check 27

What is the relationship between cultural transmission, differential association and subcultures or gangs?

However, Cohen has been criticised because only a small minority of working-class youth get involved with gangs or anti-school subcultures. Cohen's theory therefore fails to explain why the majority of working-class youth, who probably share many of the same experiences of school as deviant youth, do not engage in subcultural activities.

Cloward and Ohlin attempt to compensate for this weakness in Cohen's analysis by pointing out that the type of delinquency young people get involved in depends on the type of illegitimate opportunity structure that exists where they live. Cloward and Ohlin suggest that some young people may get involved with organised adult criminal subcultures which specialise in drug-dealing and protection rackets. Winlow's study of young unemployed bodybuilders suggests that this violent route is common in Sunderland and the North East of England.

However, Marshall suggests that such criminal routes are in fact quite rare in the UK. Most working-class youth share the values and goals of their parents and consequently are more likely to be working towards qualifications and jobs. If they do get involved in subcultural activities, it is likely to take the form of drifting in and out of what Marshall calls 'crews' — unorganised groups of young people who tend to hang around together on street corners as a leisure activity in the evenings and weekends. If the crew does engage in antisocial behaviour, it is likely to be caused by boredom, high spirits or simply too much alcohol.

Focal concerns Key values that allegedly dominate working-class communities. Miller claims that working-class males enjoy six focal concerns — they crave excitement, they invite trouble, they do not like to defer to authority, they believe in fate, they value toughness and they are street-wise.

Another subculturalist is Walter Miller, who takes a different approach to Cohen. Miller sees juvenile delinquency as a natural outcome of a working-class subculture which stresses deviant ways of behaving called **focal concerns**. These include a heightened sense of masculinity which stresses toughness and using violence as a problem-solving device, looking for excitement, being anti-authority and being streetwise.

Evaluation of subcultural theories

Subcultural theories have been criticised by feminist sociologists for being '**malestream**', which means they focus exclusively on boys and fail to take any interest in girls' deviance or involvement with subcultures. Interactionists argue that the problem of delinquent subcultures is socially constructed by police stereotyping of young people as potentially more deviant than other groups. As a result, groups of youth are targeted by the police and stopped, searched and arrested more than other social groups. Marxists criticise subculturalists because they fail to acknowledge the role of unemployment, poverty and urban deprivation caused by the unequal organisation of the capitalist system.

Malestream This means that the study of females is either neglected or ignored altogether. The emphasis of sociological study is exclusively male.

Feminism

There are two broad approaches to crime committed by women. Some feminists suggest that females commit more crime than the official criminal statistics indicate. For example, self-reports show much higher rates of criminality among girls and women (although such reports do tend to over-focus on fairly trivial crimes). This approach also argues that female criminals are less likely to appear in the crime statistics because they are treated more softly by the police — for example, they are more likely to be informally cautioned and less likely to be formally arrested and charged. This is supposedly the result of paternalistic stereotypes held by police officers who label females as less suspicious and criminal than males. However, this view has been challenged by Heidensohn, who argues that certain types of women, for example those who do not fit the feminine–maternal stereotype (lesbians, feminists, prostitutes), are treated more harshly by the courts, as are women who kill, who are viewed as 'double deviants' because they have broken the 'rules' of both society and femininity.

Knowledge check 28

Why are some women viewed as 'double deviants'?

However, a second feminist approach accepts that females do not commit as much crime as males and attempts to explain why. This approach suggests that part of the answer might lie with gender role socialisation, which socialises female children into values and norms such as gentleness, empathy, nurturance and compassion that may discourage crime. On the other hand, socialisation into masculinity may mean the learning of behaviours such as aggression, competitiveness and risk taking, which could easily spill over into deviance. Smart also notes that parents exercise more social controls over girls compared with boys and consequently boys are more likely to be found in public spaces with their peers where crime occurs while girls spend more time in the home. Girls may also be more likely to avoid deviant behaviour because they fear a 'bad reputation'. These social controls may extend into adulthood — for example, females are less likely to be out alone at night compared with males.

Carlen uses a 'control theory' approach to explain why some females might be motivated to commit crime. Her interviews with female prisoners found that many of them had been sexually and physically abused both as children and as adults. Many of them had run away and were homeless as a result. Many had turned to drugs. Carlen argues that these women are more likely than most other women to lack the controls of attachment (they feel unloved or are in abusive relationships), commitment (they are likely to have dropped out of education because of their childhood problems and be unemployed), involvement (their reputation was poor because of drug abuse and previous criminal convictions) and belief (they felt no strong commitment to rules, especially when trying to raise money for drugs). Carlen argues that these women have nothing to lose by committing criminality because they have been excluded from the normal deals that women experience, for example the gender deal (a happy childhood, marriage and family) or the class deal (educational qualifications, a career and a comfortable standard of living). The benefits of crime, therefore, for these women far outweigh the costs of crime.

Other feminist analyses of female crime have focused on the **feminisation of poverty**. There is some evidence that females, especially single mothers, are more likely to experience poverty and that this may be fuelling crimes such as shoplifting, benefit fraud and prostitution. Other feminists suggest that violent crime committed by young females is on the increase. Burman suggests that this may be the result of increased alcohol intake but it may also indicate that some working-class young females are adopting male traits such as aggression, competitiveness and thrill seeking.

Feminisation of poverty Increased divorce rates, more women in low-waged jobs, the increase in women's unemployment and more lone parenthood — all cause financial stresses for women and may fuel an increase in crime committed by women.

Knowledge check 29

Explain what is meant by the feminisation of poverty and suggest how this might help explain the types of crime that women commit.

Evaluation of feminism

Feminists, apart from Carlen, have been criticised for over-focusing on gender and neglecting the fact that most female offenders are working class. Working-class girls and women who turn to crime are probably motivated by many of the same factors that motivate working-class men, that is, poverty and the feelings of humiliation, powerlessness, envy and hostility that accompany this marginalised position in society.

Summary

- Some theories of crime and deviance blame the families or the communities in which people live for their criminality. For example, Miller blames working-class parents for socialising their male children into deviant focal concerns. Murray, too, blames parents who are part of an underclass allegedly socialising their children into deviant forms of behaviour such as idleness and welfare dependency, while other New Right thinkers blame the decline of community controls.
- There are a number of theories that focus on subcultures or gangs, including Cohen's status frustration theory, Miller's focal concerns theory, underclass theory and left realism.
- Other theories blame social structure. Functionalists such as Merton see the flaws of capitalism as responsible for crime, while Marxists blame the organisation of capitalism. Left realists, too, focus on how the organisation of capitalist societies produces deprivation and marginalisation which may fuel crime. Feminists blame the patriarchal culture which encourages socialisation into a masculine identity that may spill over into crime.
- Some theories argue that crime is socially constructed. Interactionists suggest that the powerful make the laws and are able to label the behaviour of particular social groups as criminal. Consequently, some groups exercise little or no choice in the social construction of their criminality.
- Some theories focus on the choice to commit crime. Marxists such as Gordon see crime as a rational choice in response to poverty, while neo-Marxists see criminality as a political response to the inequities of capitalism. In contrast, Hirschi sees crime as a rational response to having few social controls in one's life so that the benefits of crime outweigh its potential costs.

How can crime and deviance be reduced?

Left-wing social policy and crime

Structural changes in society

Structural changes are recommended mainly by left realists, who suggest that the economic system that makes up modern capitalist societies needs to be radically overhauled, otherwise it is only the symptoms rather the causes of crime that get treated. Left realists argue that politicians need to remove the economic and social conditions that motivate the poor to commit crime in the first place. In particular, left realists focus on the reduction of inequalities in wealth and income and investment by governments and companies in education and jobs in deprived neighbourhoods to lift the poor out of poverty. There is some evidence from the USA that the more that is spent on education and jobs for the poor, the more money is saved later in terms of benefits and prison.

Knowledge check 30

What economic and social conditions need to be changed, according to left realists, to reduce crime?

However, Marxists argue that capitalism is ultimately responsible for inequality and lack of meritocracy. They claim that the crime problem can only be resolved by abolishing capitalism altogether and adopting a fairer socialist economic system.

Social and community crime prevention and punishment

Left realists argue that racial discrimination needs to be addressed across all areas of society but especially in policing. Institutional racism and racial profiling need to be abolished so that ethnic minority communities have more confidence in the police and so that police–community relationships become more cooperative.

Multi-agency working

Another left-wing idea relating to community crime prevention concerns improving cooperation between social and government agencies such as the police, the local council, social services, the media, religion, community groups, the school and education authorities, and the family. Lea and Young argue for a more coordinated approach between these agencies, including more communication regarding individuals and families seen to be 'at risk' of offending and/or victimisation, allowing for early interventions.

Restorative justice

Braithwaite (1989) suggests there are two types of shaming available to the criminal justice system. The most commonly used is **disintegrative shaming**, which involves the replacement of an offender's usual set of statuses (for example, mother, father, son, daughter, worker and so on) with the master status of 'criminal' or 'ex-con', which shapes all future interactions with that person and essentially excludes that person from 'normal' society. For example, when a person comes out of prison, they may still be treated as a criminal and shunned by family and friends, and discriminated against by employers and the police. The status they occupied before being found guilty of a criminal offence has totally disintegrated.

Disintegrative shaming An interactionist concept because it is a type of negative labelling.

However, Braithwaite argues that disintegrative shaming should be replaced with re-integrative shaming, in which the deviant act — a bad thing — is shamed rather than the individual who commits it, that is, the notion of a bad person should be abandoned (and, with it, the master status of criminal). Braithwaite argues that the focus should be on helping the offender to realise that bad things have negative consequences for others. This approach is referred to as restorative justice. For example, this might involve a meeting between offenders and victims, in which the latter could explain how the bad thing has negatively affected them and in which the former could express remorse for their actions. This makes it easier for the victim, the offender and the community to separate the offender from the offence, to forgive them and to re-integrate the wrongdoer back into mainstream society. If the offender is not negatively labelled and discriminated against, this may prevent their involvement in criminal subcultures and further crime.

Knowledge check 31

Explain what is meant by restorative justice and give an example.

Knowledge check 32

How might the New Right criticise the idea of re-integrative shaming?

Right-wing social policy and crime

Murray argued that crime could be reduced only if welfare payments to the poor were reduced or abolished altogether in order to motivate members of the underclass to seek legitimate work. There is little evidence for Murray's ideas though there is a great deal of political support for them — hence, the Conservative government's Troubled Families programme and **austerity cuts**, which have hit the poorest sections of society the hardest.

Austerity cuts Refer to the severe cuts in public spending, especially in the field of welfare, in order to bring down the national debt.

Situational crime prevention

Situational crime prevention (SCP) policies focus on increasing the costs or risks in a particular situation so that the benefits of crime are significantly reduced. They include the following:

- **Designing out crime or target hardening.** Right-wing views tend to focus on the individual taking more responsibility for their welfare and homes. In this view, it is the responsibility of the householder, the car owner and businesses to take action against the criminal by designing crime out of their lives through investing in security systems — for example, locks for doors and windows, surveillance cameras, and the installation of alarms and security lights. Individuals are therefore being encouraged to make themselves harder targets.
- **CCTV.** The UK has the highest number of CCTV cameras in the Western world — an estimated 4.2 million, which is one for every fourteen people.

However, some criminologists are critical of SCP policies for six reasons:

- These strategies over-focus on street crimes and burglary, and ignore white-collar, corporate and state crimes which are more costly and harmful.
- Most crime is probably **opportunistic** and fuelled by alcohol and drugs rather than taking place after a rational weighing-up of the costs and benefits of crime.
- The root causes of crime such as poverty and inequality are ignored.
- Surveillance infringes people's right to privacy.
- Surveillance may also be guilty of stereotyping and negative labelling because it tends to focus disproportionately on young males or black people.
- SCP may displace crime rather than reduce it because criminals deterred by tough security simply move to where the security does not exist. This often means moving to working-class areas where people cannot afford to invest in security.

Opportunistic crime Refers to crime committed on the spur of the moment, as the opportunity presented itself. It is an unplanned spontaneous act.

Knowledge check 33

How does situational crime prevention increase the costs of crime?

Environmental crime prevention

Environmental crime prevention (ECP) is also based on right-wing ideas, especially Wilson's broken windows theory. Wilson suggests that environmental deterioration sends out the message that the community does not care what happens to the neighbourhood which attracts more antisocial and deviant elements. In order to avoid this, ECP recommends the following:

- The authorities need to take more responsibility for improving local neighbourhoods by repairing broken windows, cleaning graffiti, towing away abandoned cars and so on.
- Neighbourhoods should be flooded with police officers, who should be encouraged to be intolerant of any deviant or criminal activity including antisocial behaviour, aggressive begging, dealing in and open use of drugs, being drunk in public, graffiti, dog fouling, littering and vandalism. This aggressive policing policy is known as zero tolerance and is aimed at increasing the certainty of capture, thereby making the cost of crime greater than any benefit. Wilson believed that zero-tolerance policing would result in communities taking more responsibility for the informal policing of their neighbourhoods. Such policies were supposedly responsible for the massive decrease in crime in New York in the 1990s.

However, two criticisms of ECP are worth highlighting. First, it overemphasises the control of disorder, rather than tackling what left realists see as the underlying causes of neighbourhood decline, such as governments and businesses failing to invest money in inner-city areas or tackle poverty, or even the criminogenic nature of capitalism. Second, zero tolerance encourages the police to stereotype and discriminate against what it sees as 'problem groups', which on the basis of past experience are likely to be members of ethnic minorities, the poor and the homeless.

Retributive justice

Retribution means 'paying back' via punishment. Some right-wing sociologists argue that one of the reasons crime increased in the latter half of the twentieth century was that punishment, particularly prison, was regarded by criminals as too soft and therefore it had lost its deterrence value.

Van den Haag argues that the criminal justice system needs to be harder, that is, more punitive and retributive, in terms of both the length of prison sentences and the actual experience of imprisonment. The best examples of this sort of approach are to be found in the USA — many US states have capital punishment and prisoners have to do 'hard labour', for example breaking rocks or working in the fields, as part of their prison programme.

Retributive justice Refers to the idea that the punishment should be proportionate to the offence and that the offender needs to forfeit something, for example freedom, in return for the harm or damage done by their crime.

Punitive punishment and control

Van den Haag argues that if criminals can clearly see that if they are caught they will receive long prison sentences, they will see that the costs always outweigh the benefits and this will deter future crime. Van den Haag recommended the adoption of the 'three strikes and you're out' policy (established in California), in which offenders are jailed for life for a third offence, whatever it is. He also recommended that parents who could not control their children should be sent to prison.

The retributive approach is based on the idea that 'prison works' because fear of it increases the cost of crime in terms of losing one's freedom. It is also suggested that prison works because it takes criminals off the streets.

However, despite the UK locking up over 80,000 people in 2012, there is little evidence that prison works. Left realist Matthews notes that they often act as 'universities of crime' and that they are often an expensive way of making bad people worse. Moreover, about two-thirds of people in prison reoffend when they are released. Matthews suggests that a large proportion of prisoners need treatment (for mental illness and drug addiction) rather than punishment. The anti-retribution argument suggests reform and rehabilitation through education, training for jobs, anger management and restorative justice are better for ensuring prisoners do not return to crime.

Knowledge check 34

Why are prisons described as universities of crime?

Summary

- Left-wing theories which blame the social structure for crime tend to suggest that if policies that improve educational or employment opportunities for the poor, or which increase economic investment in deprived areas, are introduced, these will eventually reduce crime rates.
- Left-wing interactionist theories highlight the need to rid the police of institutional racism to improve community–police relations and the need to rid the criminal of the stigma associated with crime so that they can re-integrate back into the community without suffering prejudice and discrimination.
- Right-wing theories argue that the costs of crime for the criminal need to exceed the benefits of crime. They argue that there needs to be more personal and community responsibility for and investment in designing out crime, as well as more police on the streets, so that criminals are deterred from committing crime in the first place.
- New Right sociologists also believe in the power of punishment, which they argue has been too soft in the past. They believe in retributive justice and increasing the cost of crime so that it always outweighs the benefits.

Questions & Answers

How to use this section

In this section you will find three questions at A-level. Each has an A-grade answer with comments on each answer at the end, stating why it gained the marks it did, and what improvements, if any, could be made. The question numbering for the A-level questions is the same as you will find in the examination.

You should read each question carefully, and either try to answer it in full or at least make notes of how you would answer it *before* reading the student answer and comments. This might help to pick up on mistakes you have made or things that you are doing well. Remember that there is no single perfect way of answering an exam question — the highest marks can be gained by taking different approaches, especially in the higher-mark questions. However, the comments should help to show you the kinds of approach that would do well, and some of the pitfalls to avoid.

As a general point, you should always read through the whole question before starting to write. When you come to answer the question that is based on a source, read the source particularly carefully, as it will contain material that is essential to answering the question.

Examiner comments on the questions are preceded by the icon e and give hints and guidance on how to answer the question. The candidate answers are also accompanied by comments. These are preceded by the icon e and indicate where credit is due. The comments tell you what it is that enables the candidate to score so highly. Particular attention is given to the candidate's use of the examinable skills or Assessment Objectives (AOs): AO1, knowledge and understanding (including range and depth of relevant sociological evidence); AO2, application (relating to how well focused the answer is, and/or how well the source has been applied); and AO3, analysis and evaluation (relating to criticisms and challenges to the view in the question, and including a reasoned conclusion for some questions). You should already be familiar with these from your other two components.

The A-level examination

The topic of 'Debates in contemporary society' is examined on Paper 3 of the A-level examination, which is organised into two sections. Section A, which is compulsory, focuses on 'Globalisation and the digital social world' and contains two sources. Both sources contain information about aspects of the topic that must be used to answer questions 1 and 2, in addition to wider sociological knowledge where appropriate. Question 3 will solely depend on your wider sociological knowledge. Section A questions add up to 35 marks altogether or 33% of the paper.

Section B comprises questions on the three optional units. This guide focuses on one of these — Crime and deviance — which is Option 1. It will contain three questions, which must all be answered, worth 10, 20 and 40 marks respectively. Section B questions therefore add up to 70 marks altogether or 67% of the paper.

The whole exam lasts for 2 hour 15 minutes, carries 105 marks and is worth 35% of the A-level qualification. It is worth spending about 45 minutes on Section A and 90 minutes on Section B. Try to manage your time so that you have enough spare to read through your responses to the whole paper at the end.

Question 1

Section A

Globalisation and the digital social world

Read the source material and answer all the questions in Section A.

Source A

Globalisation is the term used to refer to the integration of goods, services, and culture among the nations of the world. Advances in telecommunication technologies have particularly accelerated globalisation. In 2012, the internet was being used in over 150 countries by 2.4 billion people worldwide. From the development of the World Wide Web in the 1990s to the social networks and e-commerce of today, the internet has continued to increase integration between countries, making globalisation a fact of life for citizens all over the world.

Source B

As the digital revolution continues to spread across the world, it is also creating a separation between those who have access to this global network and those who do not. This digital divide is causing great concern. Certain social categories — low-income households, senior citizens, children from lone-parent families, the undereducated and underqualified and members of ethnic minority groups — are prevented from receiving fair access to digital communication technology. Moreover, this digital divide can also occur between regions in the same country. There is also a global digital divide. For example, although mobile phone technology has dramatically expanded in Africa, broadband connections are extremely poor compared with Western societies.

1 With reference to the sources, explain how digital communications have contributed to the process of globalisation. [9 marks]

ⓔ You must make clear reference to the sources as well as your wider knowledge.

2 With reference to the sources, to what extent has the digital divide weakened the idea that the world has experienced a digital revolution? [10 marks]

ⓔ You need to supplement reference to the sources with your wider knowledge. The phrase 'to what extent' means you are expected to include some evaluation of the statement.

3 Evaluate the view that the world has become a global village characterised by cultural homogeneity or sameness. [16 marks]

ⓔ The third question in Section A of the exam may well ask you to evaluate/discuss or assess a 'view'. The 'view' may refer to a theoretical view, or a particular side in a debate. Identify the theory and/or evidence which supports the view and then explain it. Evaluation requires discussion of strengths and weaknesses, and using evidence that challenges the view presented.

Section B

Answer all the questions in Section B.

Crime and deviance

4 Outline some of the issues relating to global organised crime. [10 marks]

ⓔ In order to get into the top band of the marking scheme, a range of issues must be identified and discussed in detail, which could include difficulties in defining, measuring and enforcing global organised crime.

5 To what extent is there a relationship between crime and the working class? [20 marks]

ⓔ The phrase 'to what extent' is asking you to consider a range of material that supports or challenges the relationship. Illustration with reference to sociological studies will be rewarded with marks for application. Evaluation in terms of a range of strengths and weaknesses is necessary too.

6 Outline and evaluate realist explanations of crime and deviance. [40 marks]

ⓔ This essay requires you to outline in detail both left and right realist explanations for crime, including studies, concepts and possibly some link to some solutions. Illustration with examples is vital to get into the top band of the marking scheme, though the focus should be on explanations throughout. Evaluation, too, must consider a range of strengths and weaknesses, and use alternative ways of explaining crime and deviance to criticise realist explanations.

Student answer

Section A

1 Globalisation means that the world we live in feels smaller and is more interconnected. A huge contributor to this are advances in digital communication which mean that geographical distance and time are no longer important. Harvey argues that this space–time compression is the most important aspect of globalisation. The internet, e-mails, texting and smartphones have transformed relationships across the world because information can be transmitted instantaneously to all destinations at all times.

Source A suggests that the internet has, at the very least, accelerated the pace of globalisation. In the pre-digital age, communication usually meant coming into contact with physical things such as people, letters, newspapers or telephones. In contrast, communication in the digital age is no longer constrained by the physical. It can now take place instantly in cyberspace via e-mails, Skype messaging, social networking sites such as Facebook and Twitter and virtual communities. Source A provides evidence of the global use of the internet — pointing out that it is used in over 150 countries, which clearly increases integration between countries.

Some sociologists are very excited by the relationship between globalisation and digital technology because they argue that it has resulted in a participatory global culture in which the people of the world can share their experiences, share cultural ideas about personal identity and provide social capital in the form of support networks.

More negatively, globalisation has been viewed as an unequal process, for example by Marxists, in the sense that it often involves richer nations imposing their culture on poorer ones: a form of cultural imperialism. This links to Source B, which refers to the global digital divide. This could imply that digital communications have contributed to globalisation by spreading Western cultural ideas globally, and that as the access to these is also unequal, global inequality is furthered.

e This answer shows excellent understanding of the question, and is very focused. It shows good use of both sources, describes more than one view and is backed up with wider sociological evidence. Note that it is not necessary to use both sources to gain full marks, but one of them must be used explicitly. **9/9 marks awarded (AO1 5/5, AO2 4/4).**

2 One of the key ideas about the world experiencing a digital revolution is that it is a democratic process and information is freely available to all, creating a global village. It is argued that digital technology has transformed the relationship between ordinary people and political elites, and that the internet in particular contains all the knowledge required to challenge the power of the state by organising global collective action.

Castells talks about a networked global society in which the politically motivated are increasingly going online and organising via social media such as Twitter and Facebook. Information is also freely available to all via sites such as Wikipedia, while sites such as WikiLeaks have allowed ordinary people to read about the secrets kept from people by governments across the world.

However, the idea that there has been a global digital revolution is undermined by inequalities in access and use of digital technology. There is a digital divide, which is discussed in Source B. This means that many people are unable to participate in this networked global society. Helsper notes that in the UK access to the internet, broadband and smartphones is often not possible for poorer sections of society such as the long-term unemployed, pensioners and the poor. These ideas are supported by Source B, which also highlights other groups who may be part of this digital underclass, including children from lone-parent families, the undereducated and underqualified, and members of ethnic minority groups. Consequently internet and smartphone use is mainly dominated by the middle classes.

However, the biggest digital divide, referred to in Source B as the global digital divide, is that which can be seen between countries. In 2014, 4 billion people, almost 60% of the world's population, had no access to the internet. The use of digital technology is dominated by Western societies because these countries are mainly responsible for the design of the software and the construction of networking sites. Moreover, most of the internet is in English, which is going to disadvantage those who do not speak English as a first language.

There is a huge digital divide between Africa and the West. Broadband and wireless access is very poor across Africa. Only a fifth of Africans had access to a smartphone in 2016 and only 7% of Africans can get online.

In conclusion, though the digital revolution has had a global impact and changed the way in which we interact, it has clearly not affected the whole world in the same way, so it is significantly undermined by problems with the digital divide.

e The student has written a well-organised answer, which explores a number of ways in which the digital divide has undermined a digital revolution, drawing from the source and elsewhere. A succinct conclusion rounds it off. **10/10 marks awarded (AO1 4/4, AO2 2/2, AO3 4/4).**

3 The idea of cultural sameness was originally identified by McLuhan, who even before the digital revolution was anxious that the globalisation of media, especially Hollywood films, was producing cultural homogeneity. Modern-day theories of globalisation share this concern. Seabrook, for example, argues that globalisation is a form of cultural imperialism which uses digital forms of communication to impose the same cultural ideas and products on the minds and everyday behaviour of the people of very different societies. It can be said that globalisation is actually Westernisation or even Americanisation, and that all cultures are becoming clones of US culture.

Marxists too are very concerned about cultural sameness and see it as a form of cultural imperialism through which capitalist ideology is spread. They argue that globalisation has been going on for centuries and is an aspect of the logic of capitalism, which is always attempting to expand its markets in search of profit. From a Marxist perspective, digital forms of communication have speeded up this process and created the mistaken impression that the power of individuals is being increased. Cornford and Robins argue that digital media is owned and controlled by a few large companies which present a uniform set of conservative values.

Marxists agree that cultural imperialism is a problem, seeing it as a form of ideology which aims to encourage consumption of Western cultural products and so distract attention away from the inequalities that tend to accompany capitalism in terms of wealth and income. So from this perspective, the media, including digital media, can be seen as one of Althusser's ideological state apparatuses, a tool to maintain ideological control. McChesney claims that social networking sites have colonised the minds of people across the world in order to encourage consumption of Western cultural and digital products and this has crowded out local cultural products. Marxists believe that this cultural sameness is a problem because it encourages conformity and false consciousness, which help to suppress protest and dissent.

However, Hall recognised that an alternative response to globalisation may be cultural resistance or defence. Some argue that some societies such as France, Iran and China have used digital technology to defend their cultures from global, and especially Western, influences although China can be criticised for overprotecting its citizens because it controls all search engines and censors web content. Iran closely monitors social media use and in 2015 prosecuted and imprisoned several young people who had uploaded to the internet a video of themselves dancing to Pharrell Williams's 'Happy'. However, there is also evidence that Africans across the continent are using digital media in culturally supportive and defensive ways in business, healthcare, education and agriculture. The reaction against homogenisation does not always come from governments. Many individuals and groups within societies may also feel uneasy about globalisation and the loss of cultural distinctiveness which it is perceived to entail, and may react in a culturally defensive way. This could partly explain the vote to leave the EU in the UK in 2016.

Other sociologists note that the power of digital media to impose cultural sameness is exaggerated. Cultural globalisation is often mistaken for full-blown globalisation but there is little sign that traditional cultural institutions such as religions and families are being overwhelmed by global influences. They point out that cultural traffic is two way rather than one way and that Western societies have benefited from the cultures of other societies — for example, Asian culture has had a significant influence on British culture. Many cultures are only selectively influenced by global culture. They select what pleases them and adapt it to local needs. This localisation, or glocalisation, produces a hybridised popular culture — for example, local people may prefer a mixture of locally and globally produced music, and local musicians may fuse these genres into new forms.

In conclusion, the argument that the global village is characterised by cultural homogeneity is only partially true. The distinct aspects of cultures around the world are still clearly evident, which many would see as a good thing, though cultural differences can also create problems.

e This answer displays very good knowledge and understanding, which is well applied to the question. A well-balanced debate is created, with both sociological evidence and contemporary examples. **16/16 marks awarded (AO1 4/4, AO2 4/4, AO3 8/8).**

Section B

4 One issue relating to global organised crime is its definition. It is usually seen as involving criminal activities that cross international boundaries, and which are carried out by organised gangs or networks. This term includes many different activities, such as international drug and people trafficking and arms trading, but can also include cybercrime and even government corruption. It can be carried out by very large-scale organisations, or by smaller gangs cooperating between countries.

Another issue is that because it crosses borders, it is difficult to police and even to measure. It is estimated that it may be worth $870 billion in the USA alone, but these estimates are hard to prove because, by its nature, global organised crime operates in the 'shadow economy', and if it is not exposed it cannot be accurately measured. Gastrow argues that organised crime today runs less like the stereotypical mafia, and much more like an international business, which often has links to more legitimate businesses and even governments, which may help cover its tracks.

Policing organised crime requires international cooperation, but differences in laws between countries makes enforcement very difficult. Radical criminologists argue that global organised crimes are committed by powerful people, who use their influence to influence lawmakers and avoid punishment. Castells agrees, arguing that organised crime networks cooperate with each other, like multinational companies, in order to minimise risks and maximise profits. However, it is also argued that local crime networks operate differently, so that the international drug trade, for example, may look different in South American countries than in Africa, due to cultural, political and legal differences. Hobbs and Dunningham give the example that drug crime in the UK is 'glocal' in character, meaning that it is locally based but with global connections. This local impact on a global issue is referred to as 'glocalisation', as put forward by Robertson.

e This answer includes a range of issues, supported with evidence such as examples, studies and figures. Note that no AO3 Analysis and Evaluation marks are available for this question, but presenting issues or problems in a critical way can be credited as knowledge (AO1). **10/10 marks awarded (AO1 6/6, AO2 4/4).**

5 It is difficult to measure the relationship between crime and social class because the social class of offenders is not recorded by the police or courts. However, prison statistics do suggest that most people convicted and in prison are from manual working-class backgrounds or come from the most economically deprived areas of the UK.

Merton argues that the working class and the poor experience a gap between the cultural goal of material success and the institutional means available to achieve that success. This strain between goals and means results in anomie or frustration for some and they innovate. They adopt criminal means to earn high incomes. For example, they may make money through dealing drugs or committing burglaries. However, Merton does acknowledge that most working-class and poor people actually just get on with their lives despite disappointment and conform to the law.

However, Merton's theory only focuses on economic crime — it does not explain working-class violent crime. Second, he fails to explain why those whose opportunities are not blocked, such as white-collar and corporate criminals, also turn to crime.

Gordon, a Marxist, may agree that there is a relationship between class and crime. He identifies three reasons why some working-class people may turn to crime. First, he argues that crime is a rational and realistic response to the class inequalities found in the capitalist system, such as poverty. Second, he argues that capitalism is criminogenic in that it actually encourages working-class crime. He argues that the dominant ideology of capitalism strongly encourages values such as competition, consumerism, individualism and greed that results in self-seeking criminal behaviour. Third, Gordon argues that inequality leads to feelings of envy, hostility, frustration and failure. He says that it is surprising that so few working-class people commit crime considering the oppressive, alienating and unequal nature of capitalism.

However, interactionist Becker argues that the working class is no more deviant than any other social group but working-class people are labelled as such by powerful social groups who make the laws and control agents of social control such as the police and judiciary. Consequently, they are stopped, arrested and convicted more. Criminal statistics may reflect the prejudices of the establishment and its agents rather than working-class criminality, therefore the relationship between class and crime is socially constructed and not real.

Another view that would challenge the relationship would be Box's Marxist analysis of crime. He suggests that the crime statistics show only the crime that we are encouraged to fear, which tends to be street crime committed by the working class. White-collar and corporate crime is largely ignored and not socially constructed as 'proper crime', so the relationship between class and crime is not as clear-cut as it seems.

On the other hand, left realist writers Lea and Young suggest that some sections of the working class, especially youth, feel relatively deprived compared with their better-off peers because of factors such as poverty and unemployment. Moreover, they feel marginalised or powerless to change their situation. These feelings of deprivation and powerlessness create frustration, anger and hostility towards the police and society among working-class youth that may express itself through riots and street crime.

In conclusion, the statistics tend to show that there is a relationship between class and crime, linking it to the working class. However, there are various theories that explain this relationship differently. There are also those who question it completely, suggesting that it is more to do with definitions of criminality and enforcement of the law.

ⓔ There is a good range of theoretical explanations of the reasons why working-class people may be more likely to commit crime, with some relevant evaluation from alternative views. More depth is possible in places. **18/20 marks awarded (AO1 7/8, AO2 4/4, AO3 7/8).**

6 Realism is a relatively recent approach in criminology that seeks to avoid the mistakes of 'idealist' theories, which had no basis in evidence and provided no practical solutions to crime. Realism can be split into right realism, which is influenced by functionalist and right-wing ideas, and left realism, which has its roots in Marxism.

Right realist approaches blame individuals for choosing to commit crime, rather than society. For example, some right realists claim that biological factors are to blame because these allegedly result in people being unable to control their deviant or criminal impulses. Wilson and Herrnstein considered the genetic basis of criminality, arguing that strong socialisation was needed to overcome this. Other right realists claim that offenders deliberately choose to embark upon a criminal career because they weigh up the costs and benefits of crime, and are not deterred by the possibility of being caught and punished because the criminal justice system is weak and soft.

Right realists like Clarke argue that crime is the product of criminals making rational decisions after weighing up the costs of crime — i.e. the risk of being caught and the severity of the potential punishment — against the benefits of crime. Hirschi notes that most people have four controls, or social bonds, in their lives which prevent them committing crime because the costs would be too great.

First, they feel emotionally attached to their partners and families — involvement in crime, therefore, is too risky because it could result in family breakdown. This is the bond of attachment. Second, people have the bond of commitment — to education, careers, mortgages and property, which they risk losing by being convicted for crime. Third, people have much to do due to their involvement in work, family and local community, so this bond of involvement prevents them from having the spare time in which to be tempted into crime. Finally, people are normally socialised into a set of beliefs about discipline, rules and respect for others and the law. These controls deter most people from committing crime.

Criminals lack these social controls in their lives, which means that the benefits of crime generally outweigh the costs for them. For example, young criminals have not yet committed themselves to a career, a family, financial investments and adult reputations and so are less affected by these controls. Evidence suggests that many of those in prison lacked family stability and had no educational qualifications or job prior to committing their offence, supporting Hirschi's claims.

Another right realist theory is Wilson and Kelling's 'broken windows theory', which argues that if signs of disorder and lack of concern for others are allowed to develop in communities then crime rates will rapidly increase because criminals and antisocial elements will assume the community is either weak or does not care. Consequently, Wilson and Kelling argue that broken windows, graffiti and rowdy teenagers need to be dealt with immediately by the police and community to send out the message that the behaviour will not be tolerated. This links to functionalist ideas of anomie — a lack of clear norms and values leading to more crime and disorder. These views have led right realists to suggest practical solutions to crime, such as zero-tolerance policing, through which even minor misdemeanours are punished. More surveillance and target hardening, which makes crimes much harder to commit and get away with, are also popular right-realist solutions.

However, there are a number of criticisms of the right-realist position. Marxists note that right realists ignore white-collar and corporate crime. Additionally, according to left realists, they are not considering the underlying causes of the criminal behaviour, such as poverty or inequality, which may be why their solutions are often only short term. For example, more policing and security may simply displace crime to areas in which there are fewer police and less security.

An alternative realist approach is left realism. Lea and Young came up with many of their ideas as a result of their victim surveys of inner London — the Islington Crime Surveys. They concluded that groups such as young working-class and black males do commit more crime than other groups. However, they argue that it is important to look at street crime from the perspective of the street criminal, as well as considering the victim, society's reaction and the state. This is referred to as the square of crime. However, a key difference between right and left realists is that left realists blame the structural organisation of society rather than individuals.

Lea and Young suggest that some sections of youth feel relatively deprived compared with their better-off peers because of factors such as poverty, unemployment, racism etc. Moreover, they feel marginalised or powerless to change their situation. These feelings of deprivation and powerlessness create frustration, anger, and hostility towards the police and society among young people that may be expressed through riots and street crime. Some youth may turn to subcultures — these may be positive and offer status through conventional and legitimate means (e.g. church groups) or negative and offer status for delinquent and criminal behaviour such as found in inner-city street gangs. Marginalisation may be linked to policing, and left realists argue that there is a problem of over-policing in certain communities which can cause anger and resentment. Phillips and Bowling have applied this idea particularly to the over-policing of some African-Caribbean communities.

Left realists argue that the government needs to address the problems of poverty and unemployment to combat feelings of deprivation. They also argue that the police need to improve their poor relationship with black communities so that black youth does not feel so marginalised and they advocate 'multi-agency' cooperation.

However, left realist theory is undermined by Lea and Young's failure to provide empirical evidence about the motives of criminals. Moreover, their theory tends to emphasise street crime such as mugging and robbery at the expense of other important types of crime. Interactionists criticise it for not exploring how crime might be socially constructed by the actions of the powerful and the police, although with regard to the latter, left realism does acknowledge that police racism can be a problem.

In conclusion, both left and right realists have added to our understanding of crime, and have provided practical solutions which have influenced many recent government policies.

e Excellent knowledge and understanding of left and right realism, with a good range of concepts and thinkers included. There was a slight imbalance towards right realism. This response would also benefit from a greater range of evaluation points from a wider range of other theoretical positions and a more reasoned conclusion. **36/40 marks awarded (AO1 15/16, AO2 8/8, AO3 13/16).**

e **Overall, the student scored 99 marks out of the 105 available.**

Question 2

Section A

Globalisation and the digital social world

Read the source material and answer all the questions in Section A.

Source A

Denise Carter has investigated how geographically distant individuals are coming together on the internet to inhabit new kinds of social spaces or virtual communities. She argues that people construct and live in these new virtual worlds in ways that suggest that the internet is no longer a cyberspace distinct and separate from the real world. She conducted ethnographic research by entering CyberCity, a virtual community on the net. She found that cyberspace is just another place for people to meet and that CyberCity participants are investing as much effort in maintaining relationships as in other social spaces. She concludes that this widens the web of human relationships rather than weakening them.

Source B

The postmodernist thinker Carl Raschke believes that the increasing availability of digital communications has changed the nature of knowledge. He argues that grand narratives which were written by powerful groups which explained how the world worked in the modern age are now being abandoned in the postmodern world. He argues that the rapid spread of digital communication, particularly the internet, has created a digital university in which knowledge is now available to all because of participatory digital communities such as Wikipedia, Twitter and Facebook. He argues that knowledge in the postmodern world is hyper-knowledge because it has expanded knowledge and social capital to the previously powerless and muted. However, Marxists are sceptical and claim digital knowledge is mainly ideological and very much the product of the ruling capitalist class.

1 With reference to the sources, explain how virtual communities widen the web of human relationships. [9 marks]

ⓔ You must make clear reference to at least one of the sources as well as your wider knowledge.

2 With reference to the sources, assess the view that digital communications have improved the situation of the 'powerless and muted'? [10 marks]

ⓔ You need to supplement reference to the sources with your wider knowledge. The term 'assess' means you are expected to include some evaluation of the statement.

3 Evaluate the feminist approach to digital communication. [16 marks]

ⓔ The feminist view needs to be described and explained. Evaluation requires discussion of its strengths and weaknesses, ideally using other theories such as Marxism and postmodernism.

Section B

Answer all the questions in Section B.

Crime and deviance

4 In what ways might gender role socialisation influence crime? [10 marks]

ⓔ In order to get into the top band of the marking scheme, you need to identify and discuss a range of detailed 'ways'. These must be consistently and frequently related to how aspects of gender role socialisation might influence crime.

5 Outline and assess right-wing policies aimed at reducing and controlling crime. [20 marks]

ⓔ This question requires candidates to identify some of the right-wing solutions to crime, but also to evaluate them — as indicated by the term 'assess'. It would be useful to use left-wing solutions as a contrast when considering how effective right-wing solutions may be.

6 Outline and evaluate interactionist explanations of crime and deviance. [40 marks]

ⓔ This essay requires you to outline in detail a range of interactionist explanations, using names and concepts. Illustration with examples is vital to get into the top band of the marking scheme. Evaluation must consider a range of strengths and weaknesses, using alternative theories to challenge the view of the question.

Student answer

Section A

1 In Source A, Carter argues that geographical distance is no longer important in preventing people from maintaining relationships or forming communities because people can now construct new kinds of social spaces and relationships in cyberspace. She calls these 'virtual communities'. Her research found that people who used CyberCity regarded themselves as a real community despite being physically separated from each other. Their participation in this virtual community was viewed in much the same way as their participation in their schools or workplaces. They spent as much effort maintaining their virtual relationships in CyberCity as they did with their relationships with their school friends or workmates. In other words, their online friendships were regarded as having the same value as their offline relationships, but with fewer barriers, thus widening people's network of social relationships.

Boellstorff, who researched the virtual community known as Second Life, found that disabled people who were confined to their homes by their physical impairment were able to widen their web of relationships by adopting avatar identities in Second Life.

Sociologists such as Miller argue that virtual communities such as Facebook are good for widening relationships because they are participatory cultures. They connect people to one another. Gardner and Davis, for example, observe that internet-enabled digital devices such as smartphones have widened relationships because they can transcend distance and allow for instantaneous communication. Young people, in particular, have taken advantage of such technology to the extent that Gardner and Davis suggest that young people today 'hang around' the net in the same way that previous generations hung around street corners or cafes.

Such communities also help isolated or shy individuals with low self-esteem relate to others because they lower barriers to communication.

e This answer demonstrates excellent knowledge and understanding, providing relevant evidence which is relevant to the question, with good use of the source. More focus on the question would have improved the answer further. **8/9 marks awarded (AO1 5/5, AO2 3/4).**

2 Postmodernists such as Raschke in Source B believe that digital communication has the potential to bring about social and political change especially for those who have traditionally been powerless and deprived of a voice, that is, groups who have deliberately been kept muted by the powerful. He argues that the internet in particular has transformed society's relationship with knowledge which in the past was always controlled by the powerful. Raschke argues that in the postmodern age people have grown tired of these old metanarratives of knowledge and are abandoning all trust in them in favour of participatory and democratic, digitally based communities such as Wikipedia, Twitter and Facebook, in which anybody can contribute to the sum of knowledge. He argues that the internet is a digital university in which knowledge is available to all and is being used by the previously powerless and muted to change their social conditions. Raschke refers to the knowledge available on the internet as 'hyper-knowledge' because it has extended our understanding of how the world works, it is freely available to all and it is not censored by the powerful.

Similarly, Castells argues that civil society is now better served by digital global networks which have the potential to become an alternative source of knowledge and political power that can challenge traditional sources of power such as the state. He argues that these networks have been used to successfully organise worldwide protests against global capitalism, while Kassim argues that the knowledge provided by Twitter, Facebook and YouTube played a major role in bringing down repressive dictators during the Arab Spring protests. Feminists too have argued that women were once a muted group but now use the internet to organise against misogyny and patriarchy through websites such as Everyday Sexism.

However, there are a number of criticisms which challenge the idea that digital communications have improved the situation of the powerless and muted. First, evidence suggests a digital divide exists in terms of access to digital communications. For example, only 7% of people in Africa have access to the internet. Second, Marxists observe that ownership of digital communications is mainly concentrated in the hands of transnational corporations. These companies have engaged in political censorship in collaboration with nation-states. For example, China has conspired with Google to make sure its citizens cannot freely access all the knowledge on the worldwide web. Finally, Curran argues that digital communications played a relatively minor role in the Arab Spring protests — it was deep-seated economic and religious factors that brought people onto the streets, not Twitter.

e This is a well-argued response which provides evidence for and against the idea that muted groups have more voice as a result of digital communication. The source is well used along with several relevant contemporary examples and there is clear evidence of evaluation. **10/10 marks awarded (AO1 4/4, AO2 2/2, AO3 4/4).**

3 Feminist theory is interested in analysing and explaining the persistence of patriarchy, that is, the fact that men dominate positions of power while women generally occupy second-class subordinate positions in society. There are three broad strands of feminism which can be applied.

Radical feminists argue that both old forms of media such as newspapers and magazines as well as newer digital forms of communication are engaged in three related processes. First, they are involved in a process that radical feminists call the symbolic annihilation of women. This means that media content, both digital and non-digital, show women in narrow and limited ways that send out the message that their achievements are less important than their bodies and looks. For example, radical feminists would point to the popularity of pornography on the internet, in which women's bodies are exploited for the gaze of men as evidence that digital media are merely reinforced patriarchal and misogynistic attitudes.

Second, radical feminists argue that the media have deliberately silenced women to the extent that they are a muted group. Examples would include 'slut shaming' and the misogynistic abuse levelled at women who speak out on the internet. The recent campaign to 'Reclaim the internet', inspired by the feminist ' the night' movement, recognises the problem of misogyny on the net and is seeking to address it.

Third, radical feminists argue that what access women do get to the internet seems to reflect and therefore reinforce traditional feminine roles in a patriarchal society. Green and Singleton suggest that the online communities that are most popular with women users — Mumsnet and Facebook — might merely reinforce the patriarchal notion that women should perform the emotional work of maintain family relationships. However, they are more positive about the female use of smartphones and texting, which they see as useful in the construction of feminine identities and communities.

Some radical feminists do see potential in digital forms of communication. Haraway argues that the anonymity granted by many forms of digital communication allows women to transcend their oppressed identity by taking on digital identities which avoid the negative judgements and stereotypes associated with femininity. She points out that in virtual communities like Second Life women can adopt 'cyborg identities' which are gender neutral or even experiment with masculine avatar identity.

Marxist feminists are generally pessimistic about the power of digital technology to change the lives of women for the better because, as Marxists, they believe that the ownership of digital technologies is in the hands of the capitalist class which is dominated by a masculine outlook. Capitalist companies are only interested in increasing profits. They are unlikely to invest in digital communication systems that rock the boat by questioning the nature of patriarchy. They are much more likely to invest in social networking sites such as Facebook or internet dating sites that reinforce traditional relations between the sexes.

Liberal feminists are the most optimistic about the power of digital communications to improve social conditions for women. They have actively used digital technology to empower women and to raise their consciousness about sexism, misogyny and patriarchy. For example, Laura Bates set up the Everyday Sexism project, which encourages women to share their experiences of sexism. Cochrane points out that other digital projects have focused on criticising the sexualisation of female children, violence against women and pornography. She argues that these projects have produced a new type of intersectional feminism in which women are now aware of how gender interacts with other forms of oppression such as class inequality, race, poverty, violence, religion and so on.

In conclusion, evidence suggests that women who use digital forms of communication may still be subjected to sexism, abuse and threats. Digital technology may have expanded the opportunities for feminists to put their case more widely and successfully but unfortunately misogynists are using such technology too.

e This is a well-argued, detailed answer with a good range and depth of knowledge about feminist views on digital forms of communication, supported with studies and contemporary examples. It is evaluative in tone and contrasts the strands of feminism, but evaluation could have been extended by challenging the feminist view from the perspective of other theoretical positions. **14/16 marks awarded (AO1 4/4, AO2 4/4, AO3 6/8).**

Section B

4 Feminists such as Heidensohn and Smart have highlighted gender role socialisation that children receive while growing up and suggest that femininity involves the learning of particular values and behaviour such as caring for others, empathetic understanding, listening, passivity and gentleness which deter females from acting in ways that hurt or damage others. This may influence them away from criminal and deviant behaviour. In contrast, males learn that tough and aggressive behaviour is expected of them. They are encouraged to be assertive, dominant and to take risks. These sorts of traits can quite easily be transformed into criminal behaviour such as violence and rape. Smart suggests that parents exert more control over their daughters, not allowing them as much freedom. This could link to McRobbie and Garber's concept of bedroom culture, where girls tend to be confined to their bedrooms and are less likely to be out and about, getting in trouble. This will clearly influence opportunities for girls to get involved in criminal and risk-taking behaviour.

Lees would also support the idea that gender role socialisation is significant in influencing crime, as she discusses peer pressure on girls from other girls and boys, such as being classed a slag and getting a reputation, which socialises girls into much more submissive behaviour.

These feminist ideas also have support from other sociologists, such as functionalists, who argue that the family socialises children into the natural gender roles — expressive for females and instrumental for males, which could link to a lower likelihood of criminal activity for females. Another view comes from Messerschmidt who looks at how crime might be a way of expressing or 'doing' masculinity. He found that there is a lot of pressure on young boys to accomplish masculinity and prove themselves. This socialisation may come from the family and peers, but also particularly from the media. Messerschmidt even notes that middle-class men may commit white-collar and corporate crime to prove to themselves that they are 'real men'. He consequently concludes that crime and delinquency are a means of achieving masculine goals.

ⓔ This answer considers evidence from a range of viewpoints, including both male and female socialisation, and makes an explicit link to crime throughout. **10/10 marks awarded (AO1 6/6, AO2 4/4).**

5 Right-wing approaches to solving the crime problem tend to focus mainly on controlling behaviour. Because right-wing views such as those of the New Right and right realists focus on individual choices and problems with culture, and on socialisation as their explanations for crime, their solutions focus on ways to address these issues. One right wing approach is situational crime prevention (SCP), which refers to measures aimed at reducing the opportunities for crime. These policies are based on the right realist idea that crime is the result of criminals making rational choices to commit crime because the benefits of crime outweigh the costs of crime.

SCP policies therefore focus on increasing the costs or risks so that the benefits of crime are significantly reduced. The main SCP policy in the UK is known as designing out crime or target hardening. This has involved encouraging householders, car owners and businesses to take more responsibility for deterring crime by investing in more expensive and effective security systems, for example locks for doors and windows and the installation of alarms and security lights.

Right realists are particularly keen on surveillance cameras in shops, schools, shopping centres, on roads and in city centres. The UK has the highest number of CCTV cameras in the Western world — one for every fourteen people. Street lighting is another policy that has proved effective. A study by Painter et al. in Stoke showed a large reduction in crime in an area of the city where the street lighting had been improved, and a diffusion of benefits to adjacent areas.

However, some criminologists are critical of the effectiveness of SCP policies because they over-focus on opportunistic petty street crime and burglary, and ignore white-collar and corporate crimes which are more costly and harmful. Violent crimes too are often motivated by alcohol and drugs rather than rational thinking about the costs and benefits of crime. Furthermore, SCP ignores the root causes of crime such as poverty and inequality. Critics suggest that camera operators disproportionately focus on young males. Other criminologists argue that SCP strategies displace crime rather than reduce it. Criminals simply move to where the targets are softer, usually working-class areas where people cannot afford the cost of increased security.

Right realists Wilson and Kelling argue that signs of disorder such as aggressive begging, drug dealing, public drug use, drunkenness, graffiti, littering and vandalism need to be immediately dealt with because otherwise a clear signal is sent out to criminals that no one cares, which encourages an increase in these problems.

Right realists believe that the police should adopt a zero-tolerance strategy. Zero-tolerance policing was famously adopted in New York to tackle graffiti on the subway, fare dodging, drug dealing and begging. Between 1993 and 1996, there was a significant drop in crime including a 50% fall in the homicide rate.

However, critics claim that the fall had nothing to do with zero-tolerance policing. Rather it was caused by the recruitment of 7,000 extra officers, the legalisation of abortion and a general decline in the availability of crack cocaine. They point out that most major cities in the USA experienced similar declines in their crime rates despite not having zero-tolerance policies.

Whilst right realists tend to focus on the certainty of capture as the best deterrent to criminals, the New Right focuses more on the severity of punishment. An example of a policy influenced by this is 'three strikes and you're out', which in some US states sends people to prison for life if they are convicted of a third offence. The New Right also believes in more prisons because they take known criminals off the street so they cannot offend again. However, there is fierce debate about whether prisons work or not. Matthews (1997) argues that prisons act as 'universities of crime' and that they are an 'expensive way of making bad people worse' in that two-thirds of released prisoners in the UK reoffend.

Left-wing policies focus much more on rehabilitation than retribution, and would argue that policies such as restorative justice, which gets the offender to face up to the consequences of their crime, are more successful than harsh punishments, and have much lower reoffending rates.

In conclusion, right-wing policies are often headline grabbing and can make a visible difference to communities and feelings of safety, but because they do not address some of the original causes of crime, such as poverty, left realists argue they will never be effective in the long term.

e This answer effectively creates an argument and applies appropriate knowledge to the question. There is a good range of examples of right-wing policies, from both the New Right and right realists, as well as a thorough evaluation of their effectiveness. In some cases points could be further developed or unpacked to show greater understanding, for example 'universities of crime'. **19/20 marks awarded (AO1 7/8, AO2 4/4, AO3 8/8).**

6 Interactionists argue that powerful agents of social control, such as the police and courts, define crime and deviance on behalf of the rest of society. For example, interactionists are very critical of the official criminal statistics (OCS), which are viewed as a social construction. They believe that the statistics are not a true reflection of criminal activity and they are a result of a set of assumptions and judgements made by the agencies of social control. Some groups — young people and black people — appear more often in the OCS because they are negatively labelled by the mass media through moral panics, the police and the courts.

The primary interactionist explanation for crime and deviance is provided by the labelling theory first discussed by Howard Becker. A label contains the evaluation of the person to whom it is applied. For example, if a member of the police were to label a young working-class male as a criminal, this would happen because the police believe they know enough about the individual to apply such a label. Marxists would argue that the police can unfairly label people and make such a label stick because the police force is an organisation of power. Marxists are critical of the interactionist view, though, as they think that interactionists are too vague about the source of power and they believe strongly that the power to label people criminal or deviant comes from the organisation of capitalist society.

Once a person is labelled and a judgement is made about them, the label can then take on 'master status'. This means that whatever statuses and roles the individual may have possessed beforehand, these will be disregarded and people will only focus on the new one. This can have shattering effects on a person. Acquiring a criminal record is an example of a master status that can affect people's future reactions to an individual.

A problem with labelling as an explanation of crime is that it only applies to minor deviance. It is less easy to use as an explanation of more serious crimes such as murder. The idea that a killer will only become deviant once they have been labelled does not hold true. Additionally, there are examples of 'unlabelled' people committing serious crime. An example of this would be the doctor Harold Shipman who murdered over 200 of his patients, but not as a reaction to any label.

Becker's theory continues with the concept of the 'self-fulfilling prophecy'. This essentially means that an individual's self-concept comes largely from the responses of others. Therefore they can come to see themselves in terms of the label. It has been seen that once a person is labelled a thief or a drug user, their reaction to the label will be to live up to it and to display the behaviour expected of them.

In evaluation, other motivations for deviance, apart from reaction to a label, would be put forward by postmodernists such as Lyng, who would look at edgework and risk as the main motivations, so challenging Becker's ideas. Similarly, the Centre for Contemporary Cultural Studies, neo-Marxists, would argue that deviance could be a conscious act of resistance, rather than more passive behaviour such as living up to a label.

One of the other aspects discussed by Becker is the concept of deviant career. A deviant career may develop when an individual joins an organised deviant group or subculture. Then, they may become influenced by those around them. Such a group may rationalise, justify and support a person's deviant identity and activities. For example, if a young male was part of a gang from a particularly rough area, the gang may encourage the individual to commit deviant acts and crimes and may provide justification as to why that behaviour is correct or acceptable. When they are more likely to see themselves as deviant, they internalise the label and the deviant identity becomes the controlling one. This will then affect their choices, decisions, lifestyle and self-concept. This can be criticised, though, as interactionists assume that once a label has been applied to a person, a deviant career is inevitable, which is not always the case. Some individuals do not accept the label and may work hard to prove it wrong.

In support of Becker, Jock Young also studied labelling and in particular the meanings attached to interactions by the police with hippies in Notting Hill. Young found that the police tended to see these young people as a group of lazy and scruffy potheads and that the police brought these meanings to any interaction they had with them, in a 'translation of fantasy'. Eventually, due to the police labelling the hippies as prolific users of marijuana, around which their identities apparently centralised, the hippies formed a more cohesive group against the police and in turn lived up to the label, illustrating Becker's self-fulfilling prophecy as well as the notion of a deviant career. Young's ideas also develop the idea of deviance amplification — showing how the reaction to deviance by the police, the media and the public can make the issue worse.

Linking to the idea of societal reaction, Becker argues that an act only becomes deviant once it has been publically labelled and reacted to. An example to illustrate this comes from Malinowski. In one tribe he studied, incest was seen as deviant but generally tolerated. However, when a man who committed incest was publicly labelled by his rival, there were consequences and he ended up committing suicide. This illustrates Becker's idea of deviance and labelling because it shows that it is not the behaviour itself that is deviant; the public labelling of that behaviour makes it deviant. A recent example would be the MPs' expenses scandal. Many MPs were regularly over-claiming on expenses and it was accepted practice until it was publically labelled, when they all apologised and some were even prosecuted.

Lemert also provides an interactionist explanation for crime and deviance. Lemert also believes that it is societal reaction that causes the deviance. He identifies two stages of deviance, which he calls primary and secondary deviance. Primary deviance refers to acts that are not publicly labelled. Many people commit such acts with very little effect on their self-concept. Secondary deviance is conscious and refers to the progressive commitment to a deviant lifestyle, which is the consequence of being labelled as deviant or criminal and society's reaction.

Lemert also illustrated interactionist ideas in his research involving North American Indians. Through his research into stuttering, he shows that it is societal reaction that causes the deviance. Lemert studied different tribes in the Native American community and found that stuttering was practically unheard of in most. In one particular tribe where ceremony and public speaking were highly valued, stuttering was identified as a big problem. Lemert found that such stuttering only became a problem when it was publicly identified, therefore making the stuttering worse. For those in other tribes where stuttering was practically unheard of, if it occurred then no-one made a big deal about it and the problem would have faded away, showing how societal reaction is the cause of deviance. A contemporary example of this is eating disorders in Western cultures, which place a high value on body image and slimness. Such disorders are seldom found in cultures that do not see weight gain as deviance. This shows that it is the way society sees and reacts to behaviour that makes it into an issue, which links to the earlier point on Becker and Malinowski.

Cicourel is a phenomenologist whose ideas link to interactionism. His study involved two Californian cities and he identified the process of dealing with potential deviants with a three-stage theory. The first stage involves the police performing a stop and search based on the behaviour they have witnessed and deem as suspicious. The second stage is the arresting of the individual but this may depend on how they look and act in response to the police. The third involves a probation officer who will hold a view of a typical delinquent and will assess an individual to see if they fit the criteria. At each stage, the behaviour of the individual has an effect and this may show whether being given a label such as a delinquent or criminal will stick. If the individual is a working-class male, they may not accept that the police are just doing their jobs and may behave in unacceptable ways through all the stages. If they are middle class, though, they may be able to refute the label and show the police and those involved that they are not the person to whom the label refers. Similarly to Becker, Cicourel brings ideas of power into the labelling process — showing that it can be a negotiation.

Interactionism has been criticised by Akers for putting too much emphasis on societal reaction or secondary deviance. He notes that certain criminal acts — rape, murder, child abuse etc. — are always more important than the reaction to them. Moreover, interactionists fail to explain the origin of deviance and almost romanticise it by claiming criminals are the victims of media and police labelling. It also fails to explain the origin of the power held by those groups most responsible for labelling others. Marxism, for example, sees such power as originating in the organisation of capitalism and the bourgeois ideology that results from this. Finally, left realists criticise interactionists for ignoring the very real damage done to victims of crimes by criminals. From this perspective, criminality is not socially constructed — rather it is something very real that is undermining the quality of life in inner-city areas.

So in conclusion, interactionists do provide a valuable angle on deviance when they raise ideas about social construction, and they have influenced other theories, such as radical criminology and realism. However, in light of many of the criticisms discussed, their ideas may be more relevant for understanding minor deviance than serious crime.

e A thorough discussion of a range of interactionist explanations, including a range of studies and concepts supported with contemporary examples. The evaluation lacked depth at times, and a more developed theoretical discussion would have maximised the mark. **39/40 marks awarded (AO1 16/16, AO2 8/8, AO3 15/16).**

e **Overall, the student scored 100 marks out of the 105 available.**

Question 3

Section A

Globalisation and the digital social world

Read the source material and answer all the questions in Section A.

Source A

A Glasgow University study led by Heather Cleland Woods in 2015 questioned more than 460 teenagers at a secondary school in Scotland about their general social media habits, and in particular their night-time use of sites such as Facebook and Twitter. The researchers concluded that teenagers who engage with social media during the night are increasing their risk of mental health problems such as anxiety and depression. The research found that many pupils felt they had to be available on social media 24/7 and worried about what would happen if they did not respond immediately to texts or posts or did not 'like' their friends' posts on Facebook and Instagram. Girls in particular worried about the consequences of not conforming to these digital pressures, especially the online bullying.

Source B

Sherry Turkle argues that Twitter and Facebook do not connect people. Rather they isolate them from reality. She claims that digital technology is threatening to dominate our lives and make us less human. It creates the illusion that it allows people to communicate better and to gain social capital but it is actually isolating its users from real human interactions in a cyber-reality that is a poor imitation of the real world. However, many commentators defend social media. They point out that e-mails, Twitter and Facebook have led to more communication, not less — especially for people who may have trouble meeting in the real world because of great distance or social difference.

1 With reference to the sources, explain how engaging with digital social networks may have negative consequences for young people. [9 marks]

e You must make clear reference to at least one of the sources as well as your wider knowledge.

2 With reference to the sources, discuss the view that developments in digital communities have positively affected the quality of social relationships? [10 marks]

e You need to supplement reference to at least one of the sources with your wider knowledge. The phrase 'discuss' means you are expected to include some ideas and evidence both for and against the statement. Remember to reach a brief conclusion.

3 Outline and evaluate Marxist views on developments in digital communications. [16 marks]

e Identify the key aspects of the theory and then explain them. Evaluation requires discussion of both strengths and weaknesses.

Section B

Answer all the questions in Section B.

Crime and deviance

4 In what ways might crime be functional? [10 marks]

ⓔ In order to get into the top band of the marking scheme, you need to identify and explain a range of detailed 'ways'. These must be consistently and frequently related to how crime might benefit society.

5 Discuss the view that official criminal statistics are the most useful source of information about crime. [20 marks]

ⓔ When you see words like discuss or assess, this tells you that an evaluative discussion is needed, considering evidence which supports but also which challenges the view.

6 Outline and evaluate subcultural explanations of crime and deviance. [40 marks]

ⓔ This essay requires you to outline in detail a range of subcultural theories and studies. Development of these, with concepts and examples, is vital to get into the top band of the marking scheme. Evaluation, too, must consider a range of strengths and weaknesses, and a challenge to subcultural theories using alternative ways of explaining crime and deviance.

Student answer

Section A

1 Young people are the most frequent users of social media and they often take a great deal of care in how they package and present themselves online. Research shows that they may exaggerate the more socially attractive aspects of their personality and not mention less cool or geeky aspects such as the fact they are A-grade students or that they like school. This can put great pressure on young people socially, and they will constantly be comparing themselves to others. There is evidence that teenage obsession with their virtual identity means they are more 'me-centred' than previous generations and this is producing more moodiness and anxiety.

The effect on time use is also a concern. Source A shows that if teenagers are always checking social media when they should be asleep this will cause mental health problems such as anxiety and depression. The study also found that girls were worried about the consequences of not conforming to online pressure to respond to other people's texts or to 'like' what their friends had posted. They were very worried about the possibility of online bullying.

Brignall discusses 'current cyber-youth' who have grown up with the internet as an important part of their everyday life, and argues that due to the pervasive use of the internet, there has been a decrease in the face-to-face interaction among youth, which might have consequences for their social skills and self-concept, and lead to social isolation and a loss of privacy.

Supporting Brignall's concerns, some sociologists have suggested online interaction has reduced face-to-face interaction. This may mean that a teenager may be friend-rich online but may feel isolated and lonely because they rarely spend time in the physical company of other teenagers.

e This answer looks at a range of factors quoting Source A and using Brignall's ideas. However, it is less successful in using a range of sociological research and concepts, and leaves some points somewhat vague and unsubstantiated, thus not quite giving enough detail for full marks. **8/9 marks awarded (AO1 4/5, AO2 4/4).**

2 There is a big debate as to whether developments in digital communication have improved human interaction and relationships or whether they have worsened them. Those who argue in favour say that digital connections have brought about a participatory culture. For example, Source B says that e-mails, texting, Twitter, Facebook and other forms of social media have led to more communication and expanded people's network of relationships. In the past people may have lost contact with people when they moved to other parts of the country. Social differences may have prevented people meeting others. However, social media such as Facebook transcend both distance and social difference, having a positive effect on social relationships.

Van Dijk sees a number of advantages in social media connections. In particular, he argues that it produces various types of social capital which can be shared and reciprocated by others such as 'bonding capital', which refers to the opportunities for mutual aid provided by people with similar interests or bonds to one another. For example, an A-level sociology student might go online to ask a community of other A-level sociology students for revision materials. Bridging social capital refers to resources that might be shared among people who are very different to one another, for example feminists may use Twitter and discover that they have a great deal in common with other political causes and as a result construct online political alliances with groups such as vegans or environmentalists.

Another advantage of social networking is that it functions to micro-coordinate activity among friends and relatives especially if they are separated by distance. It may provide a social lifeline for those who are isolated, shy or disabled. It may provide a voice for groups denied a platform in traditional media such as minority groups.

However, as Source B indicates, some sociologists believe that social networking has created a new set of problems for society. Turkle believes that social networking does not connect people because online relationships are superficial and weak. She argues that online relationships diminish the value of true friendship because they lack intimacy, vulnerability and physical closeness. Turkle goes as far in Source B as to suggest that social networks isolate their participants from reality and that they are a poor imitation of the real world. For example, she argues that people are constantly on their phones checking for texts and social network updates. She argues that this is unhealthy because it produces anxiety and when people misplace their phones, they feel cut off from reality. Finally, some critics of social networking claim that it has coarsened young people's attitudes. It is claimed that online they are more selfish, meaner and narcissistic than they are in person. As a result, online bullying, sexting and sexual harassment have become more common, as mentioned in Source A.

In conclusion, it is clear there are both positive and negative effects on social relationships, which very much depend on how digital communication is used, so it can be a tool for extending relationships, but can also have isolating effects.

e This response goes beyond the sources and identifies a range of views. It is focused and relevant material is applied to the question. **10/10 marks awarded (AO1 4/4, AO2 2/2, AO3 4/4).**

3 Marxists argue that global processes involved in the spread of digital communications are merely an extension of the ongoing globalisation process, driven by capitalism. The development of digital forms of communication has greatly contributed to capitalism's search for greater profits.

Additionally, Marxists have suggested that capitalism is guilty of cultural imperialism. Marcuse argued that global culture was characterised by cultural homogeneity or sameness. He claimed that this was unsurprising seeing that popular culture was mainly transmitted by a handful of American cultural corporations such as Disney. Updating these ideas to reflect digital media, McChesney has made similar observations about the similarity of digital content and social networking. Facebook, Google and Twitter, for example, operate in hundreds of countries across the world. He claims companies like Facebook, Google and Twitter are like imperial powers colonising the minds of millions of people across the world so they behave and think in the same predictable way. McChesney argues that this 'cult of homogeneity' destroys cultural diversity by crowding out local cultural products. Marxists also dislike cultural homogeneity because they believe that it has the ideological effect of promoting consumption (the lifeblood of capitalism) and encouraging conformity. It results in false class consciousness as people are distracted from thinking critically about issues such as inequality.

Marxists are also very critical about the uses of digital communications and social media because they believe that they are ideological in that they function on behalf of the capitalist ruling class to reproduce and justify class inequality. Marxists believe that the role of digital social media such as Facebook functions to reinforce false class consciousness because such networks mainly focus on non-critical issues such as identity, entertainment and consumption, and consequently are rarely important vehicles of protest and social change. Marxists believe that those who own or control these social networks aim to manipulate how people think and to ensure they only get a narrow range of 'approved' views and knowledge. Marxists point out that most of the internet's content is controlled by a handful of media conglomerates which have a vested commercial interest in encouraging people to consume rather than criticise. Fuchs argues that corporations and the governments they support exert greater power on social networks than ordinary people and they may use that power to silence or mute those who are too critical of capitalism.

Another concern Marxists may express is the power of digital media to monitor and control ordinary people, as evidenced by Edward Snowden's revelations. So digital media may be seen as yet another form of control, both direct and indirect, linking to Althusser's ideas of the repressive and ideological state apparatus.

However, Marxists assume that providers of digital forms of communication are united in promoting a single ideology, but they are not because they are competing with one another for profit. If their companies are pushing capitalist ideology this is most likely an accidental product of competition.

Additionally, not all Marxists agree that digital media always work in the interests of the capitalist class. Castells, for instance, takes a much more positive view, arguing that digital media can revitalise democracy by giving a voice to muted oppressed groups. Some argue that social media actually empowers people, and prevents the ideology of the powerful from dominating, since opposing, and even revolutionary, views can be spread more easily. The Arab Spring revolutions are often cited as an example of the power that social media has to spread dissenting ideas.

In conclusion, it is unsurprising that Marxists may express concern about the ideological control of digital media, given its power in today's society. However, more optimistic commentators have recognised the lack of control the powerful have in terms of social media — for example, with the rise of citizen journalism and user-generated content, although the divide between the digital 'haves' and 'have nots' needs to be bridged for this to be effective.

e This answer shows excellent knowledge of the Marxist perspective, with supporting studies and examples. There is some attempt to evaluate, however this could have gone further to explore a greater range of counterviews, such as feminist and postmodernist ideas. **15/16 marks awarded (AO1 4/4, AO2 4/4, AO3 7/8).**

Section B

4 Durkheim, a functionalist, argued that because all societies contain crime and deviance they must have some benefit for society. This is what he meant when he described crime and deviance as functional. He claimed that crimes in fact serve to maintain boundaries so that it is clear what is wrong and what is right, thus reinforcing a value consensus.

This will only work if deviance is punished in some way. Public degradation ceremonies are important to reinforce the boundaries and promote social solidarity and a collective sense of outrage towards the deviant. This view helps to understand the purpose of public executions, court cases and even media coverage of horrific crimes.

Extending this point, Durkheim also noted that some crime functions to promote community because society often unites in reaction to some terrible crime, e.g. the Paris bombings. Crime, and especially media coverage of it and the trial of criminals, functions to reinforce people's commitment to the rules of society.

Durkheim believed that some crimes were useful because they bring about social change, which is a good thing eventually. For example, the number of illegal abortions that were carried out before the 1960s (and the deaths that resulted) led to politicians eventually making it legal to obtain an abortion on the NHS. The suffragettes also deliberately broke the law in order to get society's attention, so putting public pressure on the government to bring about equal rights for women.

Finally, some functionalists have argued that crime can function as a safety valve — some lesser types of crime may prevent a rise in more serious types. For example, Davis argues that the legalisation of prostitution may reduce rape, although many feminist sociologists dispute this.

e This answer discusses a range of functions. Though some good examples were used, these could have been developed more fully. **9/10 marks awarded (AO1 5/6, AO2 4/4).**

5 The official criminal statistics (OCS) are made up of crimes reported to the police and crimes recorded by the police. They are supplemented by data from the Crime Survey of England and Wales (CSEW) which asks its sample about their experiences of crime as a victim in the previous year.

Positivist sociologists, such as functionalists, believe that the OCS are useful because they give sociologists an insight into crime trends. For example, the OCS clearly show that crime dramatically rose between the 1970s and 1990s, although in recent years it has fallen because property crime has declined a lot. The OCS also identify the 'typical criminal' as young, male and, in some inner-city areas, black. This means that OCS can be useful in targeting particular crimes and criminals to reduce crime. Functionalists and other right-wing sociologists tend to accept the picture of a typical criminal presented in the statistics without question.

However, interpretivists would argue that sociologists cannot trust the reliability and validity of the OCS because they are socially constructed. This means the OCS tell sociologists more about the groups involved in their collection, especially victims and the general public, the police and the courts, than they do about crime and criminals.

Many sociologists are very critical of the OCS because they exclude the 'dark figure' of unreported and unrecorded crimes. Marxists argue that the OCS do not include white-collar crimes such as tax fraud, nor employers breaking health and safety rules. Similarly, OCS do not include corporate crime, much of which goes undetected.

Many crimes go unreported by victims. For example, Winlow argues that crimes such as hate crimes against gay people and the disabled, antisocial behaviour, rape and cybercrimes often go unreported. Also, victimless crimes such as prostitution and drug use are rarely reported. These crimes depend on police detection, casting doubt on the usefulness of the CSEW as well as police records.

The OCS can be seen as socially constructed because they reflect the priorities and judgements of police officers not the actions of criminals. Cicourel argues that middle-class parents are more likely to be successful in using their cultural capital to avoid their children being arrested. Feminists argue that OCS simply reflect patriarchal practices in the police and underestimate the violence that occurs against women. They claim that women tend to be seen as doubly deviant (where they break the law and deviate from their traditional feminine roles) and also that the police are more lenient with women on the basis of their gender (the chivalry thesis). Some argue that due to institutional racism in the police, black African-Caribbean and Muslim people are more likely to be targeted by the police. They are labelled as 'suspicious' or 'criminal' and therefore the police target them and stop, search and arrest these groups more. Therefore, OCS reflect these attitudes rather than providing an accurate picture of crime.

It has been suggested that alternative measures of crime such as more qualitative victim surveys and self-report studies are more valid since they allow people to describe the crimes they have committed and been victims of themselves. Therefore, in order to get a true picture of crime, these three measures ought to be considered together.

In conclusion, positivists believe that the OCS are both reliable and valid with regard to the reality of crime. In contrast, interpretivists believe that the OCS are socially constructed by the failure of some groups to report crime, the police's failure to record two-thirds of crime and the decision of police officers to see some groups as more in need of policing.

ⓔ There is relevant information here, including strengths and weaknesses of OCS which are discussed from a range of theoretical positions. Alternative measures are also discussed. The conclusion adds little, and just repeats the arguments — try to reach a clear conclusion based on the question. **17/20 marks awarded (AO1 7/8, AO2 4/4, AO3 6/8).**

6 The concept of subculture is really important in the study of crimes committed by young people. A subculture is a smaller group within a larger group whose values are different in some way. Here it refers to how peer pressure might lead to young people forming gangs and carrying out various types of crimes associated with young people such as joyriding, drug use and vandalism. There are several strands of subcultural theories of crime, which emerged because many sociological theories of crime focused on individuals committing crime.

Albert Cohen claimed that juvenile delinquency was caused by status frustration. Status frustration refers to the tension between the goal of all young males — which he argued is status, or respect from your peers — and the inability to achieve status through legitimate means. He argued that working-class boys are prevented from achieving status because their parents have not encouraged them to do well at school and teachers have labelled them as failures. As a result, the boys experience status frustration and form anti-school subcultures or gangs, which turn the value system of the school upside down and award status for breaking school rules and antisocial and delinquent behaviour.

However, the Marxist interpretivist Willis criticises Cohen's ideas because he does not explain why most working-class youth never get into trouble. Cohen also ignores females who get into trouble, which is a general problem with many subcultural theories of crime.

Another subcultural theory is that of Miller, who claims that delinquency is mainly carried out by working-class boys who exaggerate working-class cultural values such as toughness, contempt for authority and risk taking to compensate for the boredom of school, jobs and unemployment. Boys are therefore united in subcultures by these values or focal concerns. However, this study does not explain why middle-class boys form deviant subcultures and it is suggested that these 'focal concerns' are shared by young people of all classes.

Though they are seen as outdated, Cohen's and Miller's ideas cannot be dismissed because studies of modern gangs or subcultures suggest they are obsessed with status and respect. Many members of these gangs failed educationally or were excluded from school.

Some sociologists argue that whether kids get involved in subcultures depends on what criminal opportunities exist in the areas in which they live. Cloward and Ohlin suggest that very few young people get involved in organised criminal subcultures because these are quite rare, although Winlow points out that in Sunderland physically pumped-up and tough young working-class men are often recruited as bouncers or as enforcers by drug gangs or gangsters running protection rackets. They may instead turn to conflict or retreatist subcultures.

Matza, however, challenges these ideas, suggesting that they tend to describe subcultures as permanent or fixed. Matza claims that young people are more likely to drift in and out of delinquency. He argues that, at certain points, all young people pursue subterranean, or deviant and underground values and use 'techniques of neutralistion', where they blame other people for their criminal behaviour. This may be a more useful way of understanding subcultural groups.

However, interactionism argues that media and police stereotyping is a major cause of deviant subcultures. It is argued by Becker that police officers stereotype or label young people as more criminal than other social groups. They also argue that youth crime is socially constructed by the moral entrepreneurs such as the mass media, who manufacture moral panics about youth activity as scapegoats for problems in society. This stereotyping results in the demonisation of young people. They become folk devils. Interactionists claim that young people react resentfully to this negative treatment by forming delinquent and criminal subcultures or gangs. For example, in the 2011 riots in the UK, the media accused youth of being disorderly and violent even though in fact there were a whole range of people involved with the rioting, not just the young.

Interactionists argue that this police and media stereotyping results in the police stopping and arresting young people more often than other age groups. This stigmatisation of young people allegedly creates a self-fulfilling prophecy and deviancy amplification. However, interactionists do not explain why a person commits the crime in the first place or indeed why subcultures form among certain groups and not others. They also ignore gender.

In recent years, right realists such as Charles Murray have argued that the welfare state has encouraged a welfare dependency subculture or underclass which is made up of long-term unemployed people, especially single parents and their children who mainly live in inner-city areas. Murray argues that this underclass subculture is responsible for most crime but critics argue that there is no evidence that such an underclass actually exists. From this context, criminal subcultures emerge and thus it is argued that greater responsibility needs to be taken by poor people for their own behaviour.

Left realists such as Lea and Young also stress the idea of subcultural explanations of crime, which they see as caused by young people feeling relatively deprived because of factors such as social and economic inequality, poverty, unemployment and racism. These young people often feel helpless, or marginalised, which makes them feel frustrated and angry. The fact that they are often targeted by the police makes them feel hostile towards society. These young people flock together in subcultures or gangs to try to overcome deprivation by making money from crime and drugs. However, left realists have been criticised for failing to follow these ideas up with any research into how kids in gangs actually feel. Without research, their ideas are just guesswork.

Marxist subcultural theories, on the other hand, such as Brake, argue that working-class young men form criminal subcultures as a form of 'magical' resistance to capitalism before they are tied down into their working-class jobs. The CCCS explored spectacular subcultures formed as resistance against capitalism, such as skinheads and punks. More traditional Marxists would argue however, that crimes committed by the powerful are more significant, and that the focus on youth crime, which subcultural theories attempt to explain, is merely a distraction from the more serious criminality of the ruling class.

In conclusion, subcultural theories provide a useful way of understanding crime that occurs in groups. However, many of these explanations are now less relevant to today as they do not account for the huge variety of types of subcultures or why some groups are more or less likely to join them. Many other theories also use the concept of subculture as part of their wider explanations for deviance. However, subcultural-based crimes committed by youths are only one type of many and therefore this is a partial explanation of crime.

ⓔ There are a range of subcultural theories discussed here, with clear focus on the question. These are evaluated and compared, as well as linked to alternative theories such as interactionism. There is a clear sense of the value of subcultural theories in looking at socially based crimes using a number of relevant concepts. Some of the explicit evaluation points could have been developed a little more. **38/40 marks awarded (AO1 16/16, AO2 8/8, AO3 14/16).**

ⓔ **Overall, the student scored 97 marks out of the 105 available.**

Knowledge check answers

1 The distances between physical places are becoming easier to reach due to better transport and time is becoming shortened through instantaneous messaging, for example.
2 Advances in digital forms of communication and computer technology; ownership and control of world digital media being concentrated in the hands of a few; rapid growth in travel and mass tourism.
3 In the twenty-first century people are more likely to be organised into horizontal digital communication networks using new forms of social media, so that all people believing in a religion communicate at the same level. This is in contrast to the traditional vertical organisations of the past where you were more likely to communicate with people of a similar level to yourself. For example, the congregation would communicate in a less democratic way; there was less access to people in more senior positions in the Church.
4 That they are created by the middle class, who seek to reinforce capitalist ideology.
5 They are the same as before but speed of transmission is much greater, giving the impression they have changed.
6 The economically repressed are unable to have a voice as they are repressed by digital media owners.
7 They both perpetuate patriarchy.
8 Men and their masculine culture.
9 A form of feminism adopted by many younger women who are becoming aware of a number of forms of and causes of oppression and how they may intersect with gender.
10 The net generation refers to the first generation that experienced and used the internet in the 1990s, while the iGeneration refers to those born after 2000.
11 Regional disparities; smartphones less used; only 7% online.
12 Boellstorff found that people are able to reshape their identity and experiment with it. Carter found that people's on- and offline identity was seen as equally important.
13 Socially desirable, fictitious and using identity performance.
14 Bonding; bridging; political.
15 Being online together but without any emotionally meaningful connection.
16 Facebook was used in Egypt to schedule public protests but Curran argues that the Arab Spring was caused by deep-seated economic, political and religious factors.
17 It combines Hollywood culture and Indian culture to produce something new.
18 The statistics on sexual offences cannot be trusted because many victims are reluctant to report the offence as they believe they may be judged negatively by police offices, the courts and the media.
19 Child abuse; fraud.
20 Women do not have the opportunity to commit many crimes as they are often taking care of children — shoplifting is possible with children/within women's traditional roles.
21 Many crimes such as mugging and burglary may be motivated by the need for money to buy heroin, a drug that is trafficked globally. Stolen goods may also be sold to a global marketplace. This means there are now global elements to local crimes.
22 There are no international laws or agencies to control or police their activities.
23 Where people feel frustration as they are unable to reach the goals of society due to structural forces.
24 Poor people have no alternative means of gaining capital.
25 It doesn't address the real causes of crime.
26 Realists, both left and right, acknowledge that crime happens and is usually committed by the working class. However, right realists argue that the cause of crime is people's natural desire to commit crime if they feel that they can get away with it, while left realists argue that social inequalities are the cause of crime. They all rely on the idea that crime has a social aspect.
27 The fact that people commit crimes in groups whose ideas are shared.
28 Breaking the law and also going against normative ideas about what it means to be male or female.
29 Women are more likely to experience poverty and this leads them to commit crimes such as shoplifting, which become necessary to survive.
30 Reducing inequality and poverty.
31 The idea that a person receives a punishment which is equal to/similar to the crime they committed — for example, the death penalty for committing a murder.
32 Because it may make it too easy for the criminal.
33 It makes the crime harder to commit with therefore higher chances of getting caught.
34 People mix with other criminals who 'teach' them how to commit crimes.

Note: Page numbers in **bold** indicate key term definitions.